pretty little pillows

pretty little pillows

3 1336 08716 0157

LARK BOOKS

A Division of Sterling Publishing Co., Inc.
New York / London

SENIOR EDITOR
Nicole McConville

EDITORIAL ASSISTANT
Beth Sweet

ART DIRECTOR
Megan Kirby

ART PRODUCTION
Jeff Hamilton

ILLUSTRATOR
Susan McBride

TEMPLATES
Orrin Lundgren

PHOTOGRAPHERS
Steve Mann
Stewart O'Shields

COVER DESIGNER
Celia Naranjo

Library of Congress Cataloging-in-Publication Data

Pretty little pillows. -- 1st ed.
       p. cm.
    Includes index.
    ISBN 978-1-60059-399-4 (hc-plc with jacket : alk. paper)
    1. Pillows 2. Sewing. 1. Lark Books.
    TT410.P747 2010
    646.2'1--dc22

                                                2009032648

10 9 8 7 6 5 4 3 2 1

First Edition

Published by Lark Books, A Division of
Sterling Publishing Co., Inc.
387 Park Avenue South, New York, NY 10016

Text © 2010, Lark Books, A Division of Sterling Publishing Co., Inc.
Photography © 2010, Lark Books, A Division of Sterling Publishing Co., Inc.
Illustrations © 2010, Lark Books, A Division of Sterling Publishing Co., Inc.

Distributed in Canada by Sterling Publishing,
c/o Canadian Manda Group, 165 Dufferin Street
Toronto, Ontario, Canada M6K 3H6

Distributed in the United Kingdom by GMC Distribution Services,
Castle Place, 166 High Street, Lewes, East Sussex, England BN7 1XU

Distributed in Australia by Capricorn Link (Australia) Pty Ltd.,
P.O. Box 704, Windsor, NSW 2756 Australia

If you have questions or comments about this book, please contact:
Lark Books, 67 Broadway, Asheville, NC 28801, 828-253-0467

Manufactured in China

ISBN 13: 978-1-60059-399-4

For information about custom editions, special sales, premium and corporate purchases, please contact
Sterling Special Sales Department at 800-805-5489 or specialsales@sterlingpub.com.
For information about desk and examination copies available to college and university professors,
requests must be submitted to academic@larkbooks.com.
Our complete policy can be found at www.larkbooks.com.

contents

introduction

Nothing can change the personality of a room (or a couch, or a bed) faster than a group of really cool pillows. The perfect creative canvas, pillows don't require much fabric (hello, stash-busters!), they beg for pretty embellishment (rickrack and ribbon, anyone?), and they're small enough to whip up in a day—or less!

We invited some of the most talented designers around to stitch up the most fabulous pillows imaginable. The result? Projects that make you look at the whole idea of pillows in an entirely new light. In this book, you'll find a collection of 29 inventive projects made from some of the prettiest fabrics out there.

You'll find a range of great techniques, including appliqué, embroidery, quilting, smocking, simple felting, and more—all of which you'll want to add to your stitching repertoire. Use coordinating printed fabrics in a fun reversible throw pillow (Quick Change, page 100); just unbutton the center points of the triangular flaps in the front, and flip them over to attach to the back. Embroider a favorite child's drawing onto the front of a tiny decorative bolster (Child's Play, page 57). Repurpose those wool sweaters in the back of your closet into modern, eye-catching room accents (Re-Fab Modern, page 41). What mom wouldn't jump at the chance to make a tooth fairy pillow (Sweet Tooth, page 107) to hang on the door or tuck in the bed? Craft a thoughtful gift of a relaxing eye pillow (Restful Moment, page 104); for the world traveler, there's a handy neck pillow made from eco-friendly fabrics ideal for those long flights (Eco On-the-Go, page 46). Never forget where the remote is again (or your secret stash of chocolates) with a decorative pillow "box" (Pillowbox Hideaway, page 118) that cleverly keeps small items out of sight.

Glance through the Basics section, where you'll find the nitty-gritty on materials, embellishment techniques, and basic construction methods.

Then it's on to the projects, which are organized into three categories. Creative Stitching features all sorts of different sewing and embroidery opportunities. Pretty Piecing & Cute Quilting presents patchwork and quilted pillows. And Surprising Spins turns the entire concept of pillows inside out with wildly interesting interpretations of what a pillow can be.

It's time to grab some fabric, turn on your sewing machine, and get started with your very own pillow party!

pillows basics

hat better way to express your soft and huggable side than by making pretty little pillows? Few home accessories claim as much decorating potential. They can handily tie a color scheme together while filling a room with warmth and interest.

This chapter provides you with the information you need about tools, materials, and techniques to make all the pillows in this book. Refer to it often while you work, and you'll be on your way to pillow proficiency.

tools

Unless you're new to sewing, a whirlwind tour around your craft space should yield the tools you'll need. Use the Basic Pillows Tool Kit (at right) as your guide. It's always best to have everything on hand before you begin. Who wants to go back and search for straight pins after wading into the creative flow?

SEWING SCISSORS

Think sharp! Dedicate a pair of scissors for cutting fabric only. If you use them to cut paper, even once, you'll quickly see how dull life can become. If you're shopping for a new pair, quality is worth the cost. Give the scissors a test run at the store. You want them to fit comfortably in your grip for a lifetime of happy cutting.

You might want to consider adding a good pair of fine-tipped scissors, such as embroidery scissors, to your sewing basket. They're easy to maneuver when clipping tight curves or doing tiny detail work.

CRAFT SCISSORS

Most people have more of these lurking about than they want to admit. Use them when cutting anything *but* fabric. Don't spend too much when purchasing a pair. Scissors of moderate length will provide ease of use for cutting out paper patterns and templates.

> ## Basic Pillows Tool Kit
>
> - *Sharp sewing scissors (for fabric)*
> - *Craft scissors (for paper)*
> - *Rotary cutter and mat (optional)*
> - *Sewing machine*
> - *Sewing machine needles*
> - *Hand-sewing needles*
> - *Measuring tape or ruler*
> - *Tailor's chalk or water-soluble fabric marker*
> - *Needle threader*
> - *Seam ripper (nobody's perfect)*
> - *Iron*
> - *Straight pins*
> - *Thread*
> - *Scrap paper (for patterns)*
> - *Pencil with an eraser*
> - *Knitting needle or chopstick (for pushing corners)*

PINS

Traditional, short metal pins with small heads will do for most jobs. If you need longer ones, try pins with plastic or glass heads for easy handling.

ROTARY CUTTER AND MAT

You'll find that some projects substitute this tool for scissors. Rotary cutters have sharp rolling wheels that quickly slice through multiple layers of fabric. Popularized by quilters, many crafters now use them for most of their fabric-cutting needs. When using a rotary cutter, always use it with a self-healing mat. It will protect your work surface while providing a printed grid that ensures accuracy when cutting.

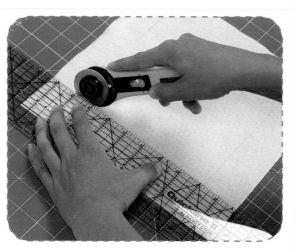

FAIRLY FLOATING ON AIR

While you can machine appliqué using an all-purpose foot, owning an appliqué foot has its advantages. The foot is clear so you can see where you're going, which is especially helpful when rounding a curve. Guidelines or arrows on the foot help you stay in line. It also has hinges, which allow the foot to float over the stitches for smooth sewing.

SEWING MACHINE

No matter how long it's been since you learned to sew, a quick review of the most basic rules for machine stitching can help you as you work. When sewing thicker fabrics or layers, make sure to reduce the pressure on the foot and use a longer stitch. This simple step allows the fabric to glide through the feeder. If a seam needs a good anchor, backstitch at the beginning and end of the seam to secure the stitching. Use a zigzag stitch to overcast raw edges to keep them from fraying. Change the presser foot as needed for the task at hand. Use an all-purpose foot for straight stitching or zigzagging, a zipper foot when applying a zipper or making piping, and a darning foot for free motion quilting or embroidering

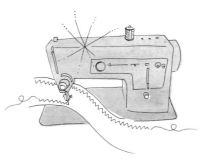

SEWING MACHINE NEEDLES

It's a fact of sewing life that machine needles always break or go dull at the worst possible moment. Why do they wait until you're a few stitches shy of finishing a seam, or seem to eerily know when you're stitching over pins holding tiny gathers in place? Conspiracy theories aside, keep plenty of needles on hand. Even if they don't break, change them often, since a dull needle can damage fabric.

NEEDLE THREADER

You're sure you have it this time. Then, once again, you miss the mark. Attempting to thread a needle over and over doesn't do much for your self-esteem. Save your sanity by using a needle threader. Simply push the thin wire loop of this tiny tool through the eye of the needle, insert the thread, and pull the loop out.

HAND-SEWING NEEDLES

Most projects call for some hand finishing. A variety-pack of needles is all you need to handle the most common tasks. Some projects call for an embroidery needle, which has a longer eye to accommodate thicker embroidery floss.

MEASURING TAPE OR RULER

Seamstresses know to measure twice and cut once just like a good carpenter. Keeping a tape measure curled on your cutting table or hanging around your neck will remind you to use it often to double check your measurements. Use a ruler for drawing straight lines or marking small measurements. It also comes in handy as a straight edge when using a rotary cutter. A transparent ruler helps when marking a seam allowance or finding a center point.

TAILOR'S CHALK OR WATER-SOLUBLE FABRIC MARKER

These marking tools aren't magic, but their lines do vanish once their job is done. Use the marker when making sewing or cutting lines and embroidery designs. The ink will disappear with plain water. It's always best to test a marker on a fabric scrap since the dyes in some fabrics can make the ink hard to remove. Chalk works best on fabrics that are not washable, such as felt. Once the mark is no longer needed, just brush the chalk away.

SEAM RIPPER

Do-overs in life are rare, except when you use a seam ripper. What's more satisfying than being able to quickly correct a mistake so you can start all over?

IRON

This totally hot number isn't just for getting the wrinkles out. It's invaluable for pressing folds, seams, and hems as you work, and you can't apply fusible interfacing or web without it.

EMBROIDERY HOOPS

Hand embroidery is a cinch when you use a hoop. It holds the fabric taut while you stitch.

materials

STUFFING

If someone says pillow, those who sew automatically answer stuffing. They know it's the one material that makes a pillow truly what it is. Standard stuffing is easy to find and great to use, but alternative stuffing can take your project to a higher level.

POLYESTER FIBERFILL

This is the all-around favorite material of choice for stuffing a pillow or when making your own pillow form (page 23). If you're looking for a green alternative when making eco-conscious pillows, try stuffing made of bamboo fiber.

PURCHASED PILLOW FORMS

These save time—and always fill the need. They come in a variety of shapes, sizes, and degrees of firmness. Some are made from cut pieces of foam. Others can be stuffed with down, a non-allergenic down alternative, or shredded latex.

DRIED HERBALS AND FLORALS

Restful Moment (page 104) provides the perfect opportunity for you to practice a bit of aromatherapy. Instead of stuffing the pillow with batting, try stress-relieving dried lavender. Try other florals and herbals, too. Tucking a sachet of aromatic pine needles inside a pillow's stuffing can recall woodland walks, and lemon verbena will remind you of summer sunshine.

HULLS AND SEEDS

Buckwheat hulls are a traditional Japanese pillow stuffing. They fill the pillow while allowing it to conform to whatever body part it happens to be cradling at the time. Flaxseeds do the same on a smaller scale. Both have the ability to retain heat and cold for short periods. If you place the pillow in the freezer or heat it gently in the microwave, it will provide enough comfort to ease a bruise or soothe an aching muscle.

BATTING

Batting, either cotton or synthetic, provides the cushioning layer you need when quilting. You can also layer pieces of batting for your stuffing. If you want to recycle material, flannel or pieces from an old towel make fine batting. If your pillow demands more structure, such as the Pillow Box Hideaway (page 118), use upholstery batting. It's firmer than quilt batting and comes in a range of thicknesses.

THREADS

You can't go wrong choosing a quality polyester thread for all-purpose machine and hand sewing. This versatile thread sews strong seams, essential for projects designed to withstand the wear and tear of active use, such as Eco On-the-Go (page 46).

Machine-embroidery thread, in rayon or cotton, adds strength and luster to your stitches when outlining an appliqué or embroidering. You can see the results in Re-Fab Modern (page 41).

Use invisible thread when you want your stitches to go incognito. Thread the top of your machine with the invisible thread, but make your bobbin from all-purpose thread. When you stitch on the right side of the fabric, no one will ever know.

FLOSSES

Some projects incorporate a touch of hand embroidery as an embellishment. Use multi-strand embroidery floss in cotton, silk, or rayon to add these decorative highlights.

IRON-ON FUSIBLE WEB AND INTERFACING

These versatile no-sew alternatives fix fabric to fabric using a heat-activated adhesive. Use your iron to press them, following the manufacturer's instructions, and you're done. Paper-backed fusible web, much like double-sided tape, has two adhesive surfaces, making it the perfect material for creating and applying appliqués with ease (page 20).

BIAS TAPE

Bias tape is made from strips of fabric cut on the bias (diagonal) rather than the straight of the grain. This gives the tape the perfect amount of stretch for skirting corners and curves when binding raw edges. You can purchase single-fold or double-fold bias tape in various widths and in an almost infinite range of colors. To give your pillow a custom look, make your own contrasting or coordinating bias tape (page 21).

PIPING

Piping is a round trim you sew into a seam. You can make piping by wrapping a bias strip around a cord, then stitching close to the cord to hold it in place. Easier still, you can purchase packages of piping, which come in a range of fabrics, diameters, and colors.

ZIPPERS

A few pillows have zippered backs; Spot On (page 81) is one. Nylon zippers are less bulky than metal ones, especially for small pillows. Zippers come in a variety of lengths and are easy to apply (page 23).

FABRIC GLUE

Use fabric glue to hold an appliqué in place before stitching, or, in the case of the Winged Wonder (page 28), use it when framing a lovely arrangement.

fabrics

Face it. Fabric is why you're here. It's all about the color, the texture, and the delicious promise of that luscious project to be. Luckily for your pocketbook, these pretty pillows use little fabric; you can easily piece together your favorite scraps with fabulous results. When selecting fabrics, you may want to first consider how you will use your pillow. Decide how important washability and durability are to you. But don't think you always have to be practical. Sometimes it's okay to make that silk pillow just because you love it.

COTTON

Medium-weight cotton, used for quilting, is suitable for making most of the pillows in this book. It's easy to sew, comes in a wide variety of colors and patterns, and is both washable and durable. Try to keep a yard or two of cotton muslin on hand at all times. Whether unbleached or bleached, it is the perfect fabric for making your own pillow forms (page 23).

FAT QUARTERS AND PRECUT FABRIC SQUARES

A fat quarter is a half-yard of fabric that has been cut in half to make a piece measuring 18 x 21 inches (45.7 x 53.3 cm). You may know them more commonly as those irresistible little bundles of colorful fabric you see at the shops. And don't forget to look for precut fabric squares. They're the perfect size for most pieced projects and for making appliqués.

LINEN

Use it when you need a durable fabric that has a bit of body to it. Linen does wrinkle, so iron it often before, during, and after sewing to keep it smooth.

SILK

Silk may seem delicate, but it's sturdier than it looks. If you plan on washing the pillow, look for washable silk. Silk has a tendency to ravel or fray, so take a little extra time to overcast any seams or raw edges.

UPHOLSTERY AND HOME DECORATING FABRICS

Even if you aren't covering a sofa or sewing drapes, you can still use these fabrics to make perfect little pillows. The wide array of textures, colors, and patterns available in natural fibers, synthetics, and blends is worth a look. These fabrics tend to be more durable and are perfect for pillows that will get a workout like the Fabulous Foldout (page 95).

FELT

Felt is soft, doesn't ravel, has no right or wrong side, and is available for purchase in just about any store that carries sewing or craft supplies. Traditionally, felt is made of wool, although the squares or bolts of felt you find in stores may be made from synthetic fibers. Re-Fab Modern (page 41) tells you how to make your own felted fabric.

FLEECE

Why do pillows made from fleece always seem to hug you back? The fabric's plush texture naturally invites cuddling. Fleece is easy to sew and durable, as well as washable and quick-drying.

STASH BUSTERS

Because many projects recommend using fabric scraps, you may be able to finally make a dent in your ever growing stash of fabrics, notions, and lovely embellishments. (As if!)

BUTTONS

A few pillows use buttons for pure embellishment, such as the Cuddle Drops (page 113). Others use buttons as a closure for the back or for tufting (page 23). When tufting, be sure to select buttons with shanks or loops rather than holes.

embellishments

These touches add personality to any pillow and allow you to make it your own.

RIBBONS, RICKRACK, AND TRIMS

It's amazing how much decorative impact you can make with little lengths of ribbon and trim. Sometimes using them is a necessity, like the ribbon on "I Do" (page 78) that holds the rings firmly in place. Rickrack, that perennial wavy favorite, brings detail to designs or adds a fun finish to otherwise plain edges (page 22).

EMBROIDERY

A bit of embroidery can spell it all out when outlining text, paint a pretty picture, or lend texture and color to a pillow. The stitches used in the projects are easily mastered. You'll find them on pages 24 and 25.

BEADS

Beaders know you can attach beads to almost anything. To see how it's done prettily on a pillow, look at Afternoon Tea (page 72).

pillow-making techniques

This section contains the basic sewing know-how you'll need to make all the beautiful pillows you want without breaking into a pillow fight. If you're a beginner, use this section to learn something new. For those more experienced, treat yourself to a quick review. That way you'll know what to expect and can get right to work.

MACHINE STITCHING

Test your machine's tension before you begin sewing by stitching on a scrap of the fabric you'll be using. The stitches should be smooth on both sides. If necessary, follow the instructions in your machine's manual to adjust the tension for the top thread or the bobbin. Now you're ready to follow these steps for sewing the perfect seam.

1 Pin the fabric pieces together using straight pins placed at right angles to the seam. Most seams are sewn with right sides together and raw edges aligned unless the project instructions tell you otherwise.

2 As you sew, pull the pins out *before* they reach the needle. You want to avoid stitching over the pins, which can dull or break the needle.

3 Pivoting the fabric when sewing a corner makes a perfect sharp angle. When you get to the corner point, stop with the needle in the fabric. Lift the presser foot, turn the fabric, lower the presser foot, and continue sewing.

4 Let the machine do the work of pulling the fabric through as you sew. This simple exercise can save you uneven stitches, stretched fabric, and puckered seams.

CLIPPING CORNERS

If you want crisp corners once your pillow is turned right side out, clip them before turning. If you don't, the excess fabric will leave unsightly lumps and bumps.

After sewing, cut the seam allowance at a 45° angle to the raw edge. Cut close to the stitching, but be careful to avoid cutting the stitches (figure 1).

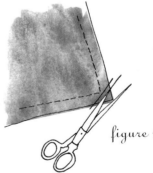

figure 1

IT PAYS TO BE PUSHY

Don't get your corners in a wad! Even after dutifully clipping corners before turning, they can still looked all bunched up. You can quickly remedy this by using the knitting needle or chopstick in your Basic Pillows Tool Kit to push the corners out before pressing.

CLIPPING OR NOTCHING CURVES

For smooth curves, clip or notch them after sewing. You clip an inward curve but notch an outward one. To clip an inward curve, cut into the seam allowance at several places around the curve (figure 2). To notch an outward curve, cut small v-shaped wedges from the seam allowance (figure 3). Whether clipping or notching, be careful to avoid cutting into the stitching.

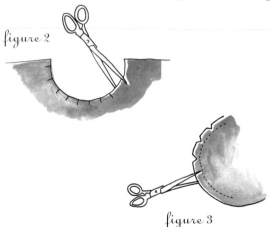

figure 2

figure 3

TOPSTITCHING AND EDGESTITCHING

To topstitch, sew a line of stitching on the right side of the fabric that runs parallel to the edge or seam. Topstitching can be purely decorative, but it has a practical side, too, such as holding an appliqué in place. Edgestitching is topstitching sewn as close to the edge as possible.

QUILTING

Quilting creates a padded, textured fabric, which always feels oh-so-soft on a pillow. You make it by sandwiching batting between two layers of fabric, and then stitching the layers together by machine or by hand. Before stitching, place pins or sew long basting stitches to hold the layers together to prevent them from shifting. For even more fun, try free-motion quilting.

FREE TO BE

If you're one to color outside the lines, you'll love free-motion quilting or embroidery. The secret is dropping your machine's feed dogs. When you do, you're free to maneuver the fabric as you please. Using a darning foot allows you to see more of the fabric as you work. If you need to stop and take a break, make sure the needle remains in the fabric. If you've never tried it, practice on a scrap of fabric first to get the hang of it.

USING FUSIBLE WEB TO APPLIQUÉ

Most of the projects that have appliqués use this technique. It couldn't be any easier!

1 Apply the fusible web to the wrong side of the fabric following the manufacturer's instructions. Do not remove the paper backing. Draw or trace the outline of the appliqué in reverse directly on the paper, then cut it out.

2 Remove the paper backing. Position the appliqué face up on your fabric, and press it with an iron according to the instructions.

3 You can finish the edges of the appliqué to keep it from raveling by using either a hand or machine stitch.

MAKING BIAS TAPE

To get a coordinated, custom look, make your own single-fold bias tape. It's easier than you might think, and can turn a so-so pillow into one that's sew divine.

1 Cut strips four times as wide as your desired tape on lines running 45° to the selvage (figure 4).

2 Piece the strips by laying one strip over another, with right sides together and at right angles. Pin them together, and then stitch diagonally across the corners of the overlapping squares (figure 5). Cut off the corners, leaving a ¼-inch (6 mm) seam allowance.

3 Open the seams and press the seam allowances flat. Fold the strip in half lengthwise, wrong sides together, and press again. Open the strip and press the raw edges into the center. This makes single-fold bias tape (figure 6).

MITERING CORNERS WHEN BINDING EDGES

This two-for-one technique tidies raw edges by binding them while making corners that are crisp and square.

1 Measure the length of the edge to bind, and then add an extra couple inches for folding under the raw ends and overlapping.

2 Open the tape and fold one of the ends under. With right sides together and raw edges aligned, sew the tape to the fabric. Stop sewing ¼ inch (6 mm) from the corner, and then fold the binding over itself to create a crease (figure 7).

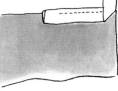

figure 7

3 Fold the binding down and rotate the fabric 90°. Don't stitch across the corner, but instead stitch ¼ inch (6 mm) in from the edge (figure 8), sewing down toward the next corner. Continue stitching around the edges and mitering the corners in this way until you get back to your starting point.

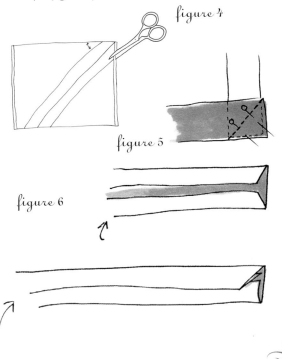

figure 4

figure 5

figure 6

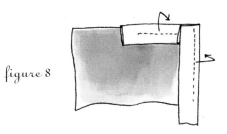

figure 8

4 Fold the loose end under to overlap the starting point by 1 inch (2.5 cm), trimming the end first if necessary to reduce the bulk. Then complete stitching the seam. Fold the binding over the seam allowance to the other side of the fabric. Fold the edges of the corners in as you would if wrapping a package (figure 9), and then machine-stitch or slipstitch the binding to the other side of the fabric.

figure 9

SEWING RICKRACK IN SEAMS

If you're looking for a fun way to finish the edges of your pillow, try sewing rickrack in the seams. The designer of Child's Play (page 57) used this technique to complement a whimsical pillow.

1 Lace the rickrack on the right side of a piece of fabric. Center it on the seam allowance, pin in place, and then baste along the center of the rickrack (figure 10).

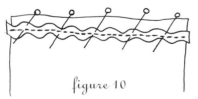

figure 10

2 Pin the two pieces of fabric right sides together, then stitch. When you turn your pillow cover right side out, half the rickrack will show, giving you that signature wavy edge.

MAKING THE PILLOW BACK

When plumping a pillow, you put its best face forward, but don't forget about the back. Though it gets little recognition, the back is the one that's holding it all together.

PLAIN BACK

Use this back when you don't need to remove the pillow cover. Unless you piece the back, it's usually cut as one piece of fabric.

1 Pin the pillow back to the front, right sides together. Sew around the edges, leaving a 3 to 5-inch (7.6 to 12.7 cm) opening for turning and stuffing.

2 Trim the seam allowance. If the pillow has corners, trim them. If the pillow has curved edges, notch them. Turn the pillow. If needed, use a chopstick or knitting needle to push out the corners. Press and stuff as directed.

3 Turn the seam allowance under at the opening and hand-stitch closed.

ENVELOPE BACK

Like the back on a pillow sham for your bed, the overlapping hemmed edges of the envelope back allow you to slip the pillow form in and out with ease. You cut two back pieces to make an envelope back.

1 Hem one edge on each of the pieces cut for the pillow back. Note: The edges you sew and the depth of the hem will vary by project.

2 With right sides together and raw edges aligned, pin the back pieces to the front, one at a time. The

hemmed edges will overlap
(figure 11). Sew around all edges.
Trim the seam allowance if
directed. Trim the corners or
notch the curves before turning.

figure 11

3 For a buttoned back, make
a button hole centered on the overlapping seamed
edge, and then attach a button to the back piece
underneath.

ZIPPERED BACK

One zip and you're there! Like the envelope back,
a zippered back comes in handy when you want to
remove the pillow form. You cut two back pieces for
a zippered back.

1 Hem one edge of one of the pieces cut for the
back. Turn under ¼ inch (6 mm) and press. Turn
under again 1½ inches (3.8 cm) and press.

2 With the zipper right side down,
line up the edge of the zipper with
the edge of the first fold, and pin.
Use the zipper foot, and machine-
stitch the zipper through all layers using a ¼-inch (6 mm) seam allowance
(figure 12).

figure 12

3 Turn one edge on the other back piece under
¼ inch (6 mm) and press. Open the zipper and pin
the fabric to the free side of the zipper with
right sides up. Position
the fold as close to the
zipper's teeth as possible,
and sew (figure 13).

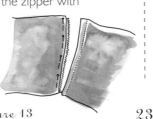

figure 13

MAKING A PILLOW FORM

This part is quick and easy. Just sew, stuff, and insert!

1 Cut two pieces of muslin each to the size you need,
adding a ½-inch (1.3 cm) seam allowance all around.

2 Pin the pieces with right sides together and stitch,
leaving a 3-inch (7.6 cm) opening on one side for turning and stuffing.

3 Trim the seam allowance. If the pillow has corners,
trim them. If the pillow has curved edges, notch them.
Turn the pillow. If needed, use a chopstick or knitting
needle to push out the corners. Press and stuff, then
hand- or machine-stitch the opening closed.

TUFTING A PILLOW

This easy finish is usually the center of attention. It adds
a bit of pouf to a pillow. All you need is two buttons, a
needle, and thread.

1 Find and mark the center point on both the front
and back of the pillow. Thread a long sewing needle
with a generous length of thread. Tie one end to one
of the buttons.

2 Insert your needle through the center bottom of the
pillow at the mark, and take it up through the pillow to
the center top.

3 Thread the other button onto the thread and bring
the needle back through to the back of the pillow, pulling it into place. Pull just enough to secure the button.

4 Take two or three more stitches
from front to back before securely
tying off the thread at the bottom
of the pillow (figure 14).

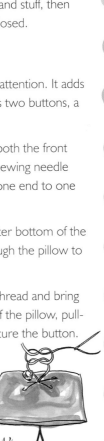

figure 14

HAND STITCHES

Sooner or later, you'll want to abandon your machine and take up needle and thread (or floss). The following are descriptions of the most common stitches you'll need for the projects in this book.

BACKSTITCH

The backstitch is a basic method for creating a seam that works well for holding seams under pressure. It can also be used to outline shapes or text.

BLANKET STITCH

Use this stitch to accentuate an edge.

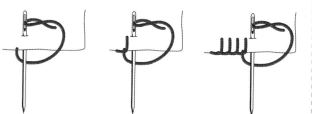

STEM STITCH

This is also known as a crewel stitch and is often sewn to outline a shape.

FRENCH KNOT

This elegant little knot adds interest and texture when embroidering or embellishing.

CHAIN STITCH

You can make this stitch to follow a line or sew it in a circle to create a flower.

STRAIGHT STITCH & RUNNING STITCH

Make this stitch by weaving the needle through the fabric at evenly spaced intervals. Several straight stitches in a row are called running stiches.

SATIN STITCH

Make parallel rows of straight stitches to fill in an outline.

OVERCAST STITCH

The overcast stitch is used to bind edges to prevent raveling. Sew the stitches over the edge of the fabric. See Whipstitch.

SLIPSTITCH

This stitch is perfect for closing seams. Slip the needle through one end of the open seam to anchor the thread, and then take a small stitch through the fold, pulling the needle through. In the other side of the seam, insert the needle directly opposite the stitch you just made, and take a stitch through the fold. Repeat.

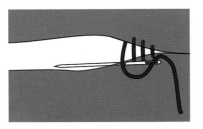

SEED STITCH

Use this stitch to fill in an outline with texture and color. Make small straight stitches of the same length and facing the same direction.

SPLIT STITCH

Make a first stitch. Bring the needle up through the middle of the first stitch, splitting it. Continue with the needle coming up through the working thread to split the previous stitch.

WHIPSTITCH

Sew the stitches over the edge of the fabric to bind the edges to prevent raveling.

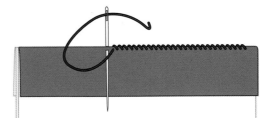

creative stitching

Whether you're adding an embroidered or appliquéd detail or simply sewing up a storm, these projects will scratch your itch to stitch.

winged wonder

DESIGNER

CASSI GRIFFIN

*T*here's no need to capture these butterflies with a net. Jewel-toned specimens of felt and embroidery are safely and easily preserved in your own fabric display case.

WHAT YOU NEED

Basic Pillows Tool Kit (page 11)

21 x 23-inch (53.3 x 58.4 cm) piece of black wool felt
9 x 12-inch (22.9 x 30.5 cm) piece of cream wool felt

Small bag of crib-size quilt batting

3 x 3-inch (7.6 x 7.6 cm) squares of wool felt in nine different colors for the Butterfly wings
Tailor's chalk
Embroidery needle

Embroidery floss in black and assorted colors

Fabric glue

FINISHED SIZE

12 x 9 inches (30.5 x 22.9 cm)

What You Cut

Black Felt
- *2 rectangles, each 9 x 12 inches (22.9 x 30.5 cm), one for the pillow back and one for the scallop frame*
- *2 strips, 2 x 9 inches (5.1 x 22.9 cm) for the short pillow sides*
- *2 strips, 2 x 12 inches (5.1 x 30.5 cm) for the long pillow sides*

Cream Felt
- *7½ x 10½-inch (19 x 26.7cm) rectangle for the pillow front*

Quilt Batting
- *9 x 12-inch (22.9 x 30.5 cm) rectangles for the stuffing layers*

WHAT YOU DO

1 Copy the templates and pattern pieces on page 129 and cut them out. Cut the fabric as described in the box, left. Cut a matching set of top and bottom wings for each butterfly, each from a different color of felt.

2 Lay the pattern piece for the scallop frame on one of the rectangles of black felt. Use the tailor's chalk to trace around the scallops, and then cut the interior felt away. Use the remaining black felt to cut out nine butterfly bodies.

3 Following the project photo, arrange the butterfly wings on the pillow front. Slightly overlap the top wings over the bottom wings. Lay a butterfly body across the middle of the each set of wings. Pin each body in place.

4 Thread the needle with three strands of the black floss. Use the running stitch (page 24) or a backstitch (page 24) straight down

the middle of the butterfly body to attach it to the pillow front. Make two long straight stitches (page 24) for the antennae and then a French knot (page 24) at the tip of each antenna. Repeat for all butterflies.

5 Embroider the wings. Choose floss colors that contrast or coordinate with the felt colors. Combine running stitches, backstitches, straight stitches, and French knots to outline, highlight, and embellish the wings.

6 Lay the scallop frame on your work surface. With the butterflies facing up, run a thin line of fabric glue along the outer edge of the pillow front. Flip the front and center it right side down on the frame, with a ½ inch (1.3 cm) of black felt spaced evenly around each edge. Allow to dry. **Note:** Do not glue the individual scallops down.

7 To assemble the pillow, thread the embroidery needle with three strands of black floss and use the blanket stitch to sew the short and long sides to the pillow back. Carefully match the corners, pin, and then stitch them together to make a box.

8 As you did for the back of the pillow, use the blanket stitch to sew the pillow front to the sides. Leave one of the short ends open for stuffing.

9 Layer the batting rectangles inside the pillow to stuff. Do not overstuff, but add enough batting to give the pillow a soft rounded top. Use the blanket stitch to close the opening.

home made

"Home Sweet Home," indeed! Using the same base template, you'll see that you can use a variety of embellishment techniques to create a neighborhood of house pillow designs that reflect your own personal sense of style and place.

DESIGNER

CATHERINE THURSBY

WHAT YOU NEED

FOR THE HOUSE PILLOW

Basic Pillows Tool Kit (page 11)

¼ yard (22.8 cm) each for fabric A, fabric B, and fabric C in complementary cotton prints or solids

1 yard (.9 m) of cotton batting

Fabric scraps in colorful prints for the windows and door

Paper-backed fusible web

Machine-embroidery thread to match

Darning foot (optional)

Tear-away fabric stabilizer

1 decorative button for the door-knob

Polyester fiberfill

Assorted buttons for the back closure

FOR THE HOUSE NUMBER VARIATION

Same as for the House Pillow, plus

¼ yard (22.8 cm) or scrap of black fabric

¼ yard (22.8 cm) or scrap of white fabric

FOR THE BIRDHOUSE VARIATION

Same as for the House Pillow, plus

Colorful fabric scraps

Water-soluble marker

Embroidery floss

Pink or red felt scrap

SEAM ALLOWANCE

¼ inch (6 mm) unless otherwise noted

FINISHED SIZE

12 x 12 inches (30.5 x 30.5 cm)

WHAT YOU DO

HOUSE PILLOW

1 Copy the templates on page 124, and cut them out. Cut the fabric and batting as one by layering the fabrics before cutting. **Note:** you will work the layered pieces as one when you sew. Cut two roof pieces from fabric A, then cut one house front from fabric B, and one house back from fabric C.

2 Fold the back piece width-wise and cut along the fold line. Hem each of the cut edges by turning them under ¼ inch (6 mm). Press and sew.

3 Pin the roof to the top of the front of the house with right sides together and raw edges aligned. Sew, then press the seam open. Do the same for the roof on the back, pinning it to the long raw edge of one of the hemmed pieces. Sew, then press the seam open.

4 Use free-motion quilting to quilt the front and roof of the house using threads that coordinate with the fabrics. Set your machine by dropping the feed dogs and using a darning foot if you have one. For the front of the house, loop and circle around the fabric as desired. For both the front and back of the roof, free-motion straight lines and/or diagonal lines that follow the roof's contours (figure 1).

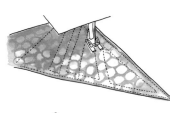

figure 1

5 Select two different fabric scraps. Use the templates to cut two windows from the same fabric and one door from the other. Fuse the fabrics to the paper-backed fusible web. Arrange the windows and doors as you want them on the front of the house, peel off the paper backing, and press to fuse.

6 Set your machine for a close zigzag or satin stitch, and thread it with the machine-embroidery thread. You may want to sample the stitches first on a scrap piece of fabric. Place a piece of fabric stabilizer behind the house front. For the windows, stitch a cross for the panes before stitching around the edges. For the door, stitch an X across the front before stitching around the edges. Sew the decorative button to the door for the doorknob.

7 Pin the front of the house to the back with right sides together and raw edges aligned. On the back, slightly overlap the hemmed edges. Sew, clip the corners, and turn. Push the corners out using a knitting needle or chopstick, and stuff with the fiberfill.

8 On the back, pin the hemmed edges closed. Place the assorted buttons along the pinned edge as desired and hand-sew them through both layers of fabric to close the faux-envelope back.

HOUSE NUMBER PILLOW

1 Follow steps 1–3 for the House Pillow. Do not quilt the front of the house, but use free-motion sewing to quilt the roof as described in step 4 for the House Pillow.

2 Copy and enlarge the number on page 124, or choose a number from a font you like and copy and enlarge accordingly.

3 Trace the number *in reverse* on the paper backing of the fusible web. Fuse the black fabric to the webbing, then cut the number out.

4 Cut a rectangle from the white fabric as the background for the number. Peel the paper backing from the number, center it on the white fabric, and press to fuse.

5 Machine-appliqué around the edges of the number. Fuse the white fabric to a piece of paper-backed fusible web. Remove the paper backing, center the white fabric on the front of the house, and press to fuse. Machine-appliqué around the edges of the rectangle.

6 Finish the pillow as you did in steps 7 and 8 for the House Pillow.

BIRDHOUSE PILLOW

1 Copy the templates for the bird on page 124 and cut them out. Follow steps 1–4 for the House Pillow.

2 Fuse the colorful fabric scraps to paper-backed fusible web. Use the templates to trace, and then cut out the parts of the bird.

3 Starting with the body of the bird, remove the paper backing and position it on the front of the house. Press to fuse. In the same way, fuse the wings and beak to the front, and then the eye and eyeball to the bird's face. Use the soluble marker to draw the bird's legs and feet.

4 Machine-appliqué each part of the bird using coordinating thread—appliqué the largest piece first and work down to the smallest. Use the same machine stitch to embroider the bird's legs and feet.

---

5 Finish off the eye by hand-embroidering the eyelashes using tiny straight stitches and the eyeball using French knots (page 24). Embellish by hand-stitching a felt heart to the front with one big X.

6 Finish the pillow as you did in step 7 and 8 for the House Pillow.

in bloom

$\mathcal{E}$mbroider your own garden, and watch it grow!
Mix and match your favorite flower shapes and colors
for a cheerful scene that brings a smile all day long.

DESIGNER

YVONNE EIJKENDUIJN

WHAT YOU NEED

Basic Pillows Tool Kit (page 11)

1 yard (.9 m) of white cotton for the pillow front and back

1¼ yard (1.1 m) of muslin for the pillow form

54 inches (1.4 m) of rickrack

16 inches (40.6 cm) of ⅜-inch (.95 cm) trim for the grass

Transfer pencil

Embroidery hoop

Embroidery floss in assorted colors for the flowers

Embroidery needle

Polyester fiberfill

SEAM ALLOWANCE

½ inch (1.3 cm) unless otherwise noted

FINISHED SIZE

16 x 10½ inches (40.6 x 26.7 cm)

What You Cut

White Cotton
- 1 rectangle, 11 x 16 inches (27.9 x 40.6 cm) for the pillow front
- 2 rectangles, one 11 x 12 inches (27.9 x 30.5 cm), one 10 x 11 inches (25.4 x 27.9 cm) for the pillow back

Muslin
- 2 rectangles, each 11 x 16 inches (27.9 x 40.6 cm)

WHAT YOU DO

1 Copy the flower templates on page 126. Cut to separate the flowers, but do not cut them out. Cut out the fabric as described in the box, left. Decide how you want to arrange the flowers on the pillow front by mixing and matching them as desired. Trace the flowers with the transfer pencil, then press with an iron to transfer them to the pillow front.

2 With the fabric in an embroidery hoop, embroider the flowers to your liking. Use an assortment of floss colors to work stitches such as the satin stitch, chain stitch, straight stitch, backstitch, and split stitch (pages 24 and 25). Lay the trim for the grass across the pillow front at the base of the flowers, pin, and stitch.

3 Following the instructions for sewing rickrack in seams on page 22, pin the rickrack to the pillow front and baste.

4 On each piece cut for the back, turn one of the short sides under ¼ inch (6 mm) and press. Turn under once more to make a 1-inch (2.5 cm) hem, press, and sew. Follow the instructions for making an envelope back on page 22.

5 Make the pillow form using the two pieces of muslin, following the instructions for making a pillow form on page 23. Insert the form into the pillow.

ribbon rounds

$\mathcal{K}$eep this polka-dotted bolster as is, or untie the ribbon closure to fold it out into a cushion. A comfortable solution to game night or take-out dinner picnic on the living room floor!

38

WHAT YOU NEED

Basic Pillows Tool Kit (page 11)

16 x 36-inch (40.6 x 91.4 cm) piece of ½-inch (1.3 cm) foam

⅛ yard (11.4 cm) each of dark blue, green, and light blue faux suede

24 x 40-inch (61 x 101.6 cm) piece of ½-inch (1.3 cm) upholstery batting

½ yard (45.7 cm) of blue polka dot cotton fabric

3½ yards (3.2 m) of 1-inch (2.5 cm) blue patterned ribbon

Thread, white and blue

Embroidery floss, light and dark blue

Embroidery needle

SEAM ALLOWANCE

½ inch (1.3 cm) unless otherwise noted

FINISHED SIZE

12 x 6½ inches (30.5 x 16.5 cm)

DESIGNER
JOAN K. MORRIS

What You Cut

Foam
- *4 pieces, each 8 x 11 inches (20.3 x 27.9 cm)*

Upholstery Batting
- *4 pieces, each 10 x 11 inches (25.4 x 27.9 cm)*
- *4 pieces, each 6 x 11 inches (15.2 x 27.9 cm)*
- *8 pieces, each 4 x 4 inches (10.2 x 10.2 cm)*

Polka Dot Fabric
- *4 pieces, each 11 x 13 inches (27.9 x 33 cm)*

WHAT YOU DO

1 Enlarge the template on page 126, and copy it. Use it as a pattern to cut two circles each from the green and the light blue fabrics. Cut four circles from the dark blue. Cut the fabric as described in the box, above.

2 Make the tube forms. Center one of the pieces of foam on one of the 6 x 11-inch (15.2 x 27.9 cm) pieces of batting. Roll the foam lengthwise, with batting on the outside, into a tube. Hold the shape while you pin.

Use long straight pins and push them down through the layers. Hand-baste using the white thread. Tuck one batting square into each end to close the ends and baste. Repeat until you have four forms.

3 Make the tube covers. Fold the cut pieces of polka dot fabric in half lengthwise with right sides together. On all covers, machine-stitch 4 inches (10.2 cm) in from each end. Do not turn.

4 Sew a matching pair of circles to the ends of each tube cover. Slightly hand gather the circles as you sew to ease them into the seams for a perfect fit. Notch the curves, and turn.

5 Insert a form into one tube cover through the long opening. Turn the seam allowance under, and use the light blue embroidery floss to blanket-stitch (page 24) across the entire length of the seam. Use dark blue embroidery floss to blanket-stitch around the circles at their seams. Repeat for all tubes.

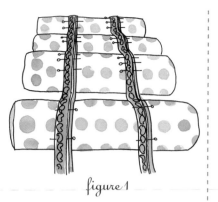

figure 1

6 Assemble the pillows by first laying the tubes parallel in front of you. Alternate the tubes by the color of their end circles. Position the tubes so the two at the center touch. Move the two outer tubes 2 inches (5.1 cm) away from the center tubes (figure 1).

7 Cut the ribbon in half and lay each piece across the tubes, 3 inches (7.6 cm) in from the ends, and pin in place. Hand-stitch the ribbon to the tubes using blue sewing thread.

8 Starting where you attached the ribbon to the first tube, blanket-stitch down one side of the ribbon, across the ribbon and down the other side. Do the same for the other ribbon. Do not blanket-stitch the edges of the unattached ribbon, which will become the ties.

9 Roll up the tubes and tie the ribbons in bows. Or, lay the tubes flat and tie bows on each end.

refab modern

Yesterday's fashion faux pas could be today's hottest home décor trend. There's a reason you've been holding onto that old sweater for so long. Don't part with it; repurpose it into this groovy felted pillow.

DESIGNER
LEESA RITTELMANN

WHAT YOU NEED

Basic Pillows Tool Kit (page 11)

Sweaters for felting made of at least 80% wool, 1 orange, 1 light pink, and 1 dark pink

Pair of denim jeans

1½ yard (1.4 m) of lightweight interfacing

7 x 25-inch (17.8 x 63.5 cm) piece of muslin

Rayon machine-embroidery thread in bright orange

Washing machine and clothes dryer

Rotary cutter and mat

1 small bag of polyester fiberfill

SEAM ALLOWANCE

½ inch (1.3 cm) unless otherwise noted

FINISHED SIZE

12 x 6½ inches (30.5 x 16.5 cm)

What You Cut

Interfacing

- 1 rectangle, 3 ½ x 5 ½ inches (8.9 x 14 cm)
- 1 rectangle, 4 ½ x 7 inches (11.4 x 17.8 cm)
- 1 square, 6 inches square (15.2 cm)
- 1 rectangle, 7 x 8 ½ inches (17.8 x 21.6 cm)
- 1 strip, 3 x 7 inches (7.6 x 17.8 cm)

WHAT YOU DO

1 Felt the sweaters by washing them with the jeans in hot water—the jeans provide friction that aids the felting process.

2 Dry the sweaters in the clothes dryer on the *hottest* setting for 30 minutes or until fully dried and suitably felted.

3 Enlarge the template on page 126, and copy it. You may need to photocopy the template more than once in order to cut out multiple shapes, as the pillow front is a series of overlapping fabric blocks. Cut the interfacing as described in the box, left.

4 Cut the pieces for the pillow front. Pin template pieces 1 and 4 to the dark pink sweater and cut out. Pin templates 2 and 6 to the light pink sweater and cut out. Pin templates 3 and 5 to the orange felted sweater and cut out.

5 For the pillow back, cut a 7 x 10-inch (17.8 x 25.4 cm) piece from the dark pink felted sweater and a 7 x 8-inch (17.8 x 20.3 cm) piece from the orange felted sweater. One of the 7-inch (17.8 cm) sides on the orange piece should be a finished edge, such as a cuff or neckline. Set the pieces aside.

TEXTURAL INTEREST

Add a variety of textures to your pillow by felting sweaters made of cashmere, angora, mohair, cable knit, or plain knit merino wool.

6 You'll piece the two halves of the pillow front separately, starting with the left side. Place dark-pink piece 1 right side up on the 3½ x 5½-inch (8.9 x 14 cm) piece of interfacing. Lay light-pink piece 2 right side up on top of piece 1, aligning the lower left corners. Pin the layers in place.

7 Set your sewing machine for a close zigzag stitch. Sew along the smaller curve where piece 1 and 2 join, catching both fabrics with the stitch. Don't be concerned if the stitching causes the edges of the block to stretch, you'll be able to square it later.

8 Flip the layers over. Place your scissor ½ inch (6 mm) from the bottom left of the seam and carefully cut away both the interfacing and dark pink fabric to reveal the light pink shape below (figure 1). On the outside edge of the curved seam, cut only the interfacing, leaving a ¼-inch (6 mm) allowance around the seam (figure 2). The finished piece should resemble figure 3.

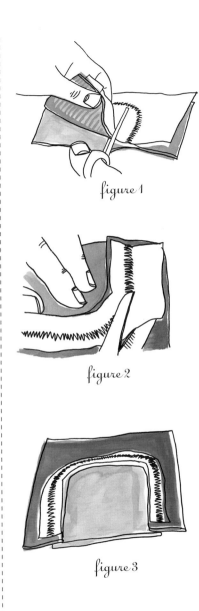

figure 1

figure 2

figure 3

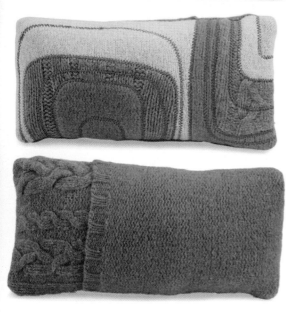

9 Place orange piece 3 right side up on the 4½ x 7-inch (11.4 x 17.8 cm) piece of interfacing. Lay the piece you made in steps 6–8 right side up over both pieces. Pin in place. Zigzag along the curved seam.

10 Make the right side of the pillow front. Lay dark-pink piece 4 right side up on the 6 inch (15.2 cm) square of interfacing. With straight edges aligned, position orange piece 5 on top, right side up and slightly off center. Pin the layers in place, and zigzag along the curved seam.

11 Flip the layers over and trim as you did in step 8. Trim the interfacing and dark pink fabric to reveal the orange shape below, then trim only the interfacing.

12 Position light-pink piece 6 right side up on the 7 x 8½-inch (17.8 x 21.6 cm) piece of interfacing. Lay the piece you made in steps 10–11 right side up on both layers. Center it, with top edges aligned. Pin, then zigzag along the curved seam.

13 ew the halves of the pillow front together. Pin each side to the 3 x 7-inch (7.6 x 17.8 cm) strip of interfacing, keeping them as close as possible. Zigzag the seam where they join.

14 Use the grid on the cutting mat to square the pillow top to a 7 x 13-inch (17.8 x 33 cm) rectangle. Trim away any excess fabric with the rotary cutter.

15 With right sides together, pin the 7 x 10-inch (17.8 x 25.4 cm) piece you cut in step 5 for the pillow back to the left side of the pillow front with raw edges aligned. Make sure to position the finished edge inward. Sew the piece to the front.

16 Pin the 7 x 8-inch (17.8 x 20.3 cm) back piece right side down to the right side of the pillow and sew. When turned, the finished edge on the other back piece will overlap it. Clip the corners and carefully turn right side out. Gently push the corners out if necessary.

17 Fold the piece of muslin in half lengthwise with wrong sides together and press. Follow the instructions for making a pillow form on page 23. Insert the form into the pillow.

DOUBLE UP

If you want to add a little more dimension to your decorative zigzag stitching, sew another line of zigzag over the first.

eco on-the-go

You'll find this pillow an indispensible travel companion. Just roll it up, and tuck it into its own compact carrying case. Made from organic cotton and stuffed with bamboo fiber, it's gentle on you and the planet.

WHAT YOU NEED

Basic Pillows Tool Kit (page 11)

¼ yard (22.8 cm) each of three complementary fabrics for fabric A, fabric B, and fabric C

Thread to match

12-ounce (340 g) bag of bamboo fiber for stuffing

30 inches (76.2 cm) of ½-inch (1.3 cm) vintage seam binding or ribbon

SEAM ALLOWANCE

½ inch (1.3 cm) unless otherwise noted

FINISHED SIZE

Pillow: 12 x 9 inches (30.5 x 22.9 cm)
Case: 10 x 5 inches (25.4 x 12.7 cm)

DESIGNER

VALERIE SHRADER

WHAT YOU DO

TRAVEL PILLOW

1 Cut a 10 x 13-inch (25.4 x 33 cm) piece each from fabric A and fabric B; one for the front of the pillow and one for the back. Note: This project uses an organic bamboo solid and two cotton prints. Since the bamboo fabric is cushier, it is used for the front of the pillow. From fabric C, cut two strips for the decorative flange, each 1½ x 24½ inches (3.8 x 62.2 cm).

2 To make the flange, stitch two short ends of the strips together with right sides facing to make one long strip. Press the seam open. Fold in one short end ½ inch (1.3 cm) and press. Fold the entire strip in half lengthwise with wrong sides facing, and press.

3 Starting with the unpressed short edge of the strip, pin the flange to the pillow front with right sides together and raw edges aligned. Stitch the flange to the pillow, beginning 1 inch (2.5 cm) from the end of the strip. Miter the corners (page 21) as if you were binding a quilt. When you approach the end of the strip, overlap the ends. Fold the flange over the raw edges and sew down to finish.

4 Pin the front of the pillow to the back, right sides together, and stitch around the entire edge, leaving a 3-inch (7.6 cm) opening for turning and stuffing. Trim the corners and turn right side out.

5 Stuff the pillow to the desired firmness. Use a slipstitch (page 25) to close the opening.

figure 1

STUFF SACK

6 Cut a patchwork panel for the sack as desired using fabrics A, B, and C with the final dimensions of the panel being 10 x 13 inches (25.4 x 33 cm). Cut a casing strip from one of the fabrics that is 3 x 13 inches (7.6 x 33 cm). Cut a circle for the bottom from one of the fabrics that is 5 inches (12.7 cm) in diameter.

7 Sew the patchwork panel. Note: For added strength, double-stitch each seam in the sack. Press under ½ inch (1.3 cm) on one long edge of the casing strip. Pin the other long raw edge to the top of the patchwork panel, right sides facing, and stitch.

8 Stitch the side seam of the panel together beginning at the casing seam. Do not stitch the side seams of the casing together (figure 1). Press the seam open, folding under the raw edges of the casing seam and pressing them under.

9 Mark the circular bottom and the sack at 90, 180, 270, and 360 degrees. Match the marks and pin the bottom to the sack, clipping the seam allowance of the sack as necessary to ease the circular bottom in the seam.

10 Fold the casing strip to the inside and stitch in the ditch along the seam line, making sure to catch the folded edge in the seam. Thread the seam binding or ribbon through the casing. Stuff the pillow into the sack by rolling lengthwise.

RAID THAT STASH

If you're buying fabric, you'll need at least a ¼ yard (22.8 cm) of each fabric to get the length required for the pillow. However, you can just as easily use fabric scraps from your stash and cut them to the dimensions listed above.

airborne appliqué

$\mathcal{F}$lying dreams are the sweetest. Let this little work of avian-inspired art send you soaring to slumberland with wings outstretched.

DESIGNER

KAJSA WIKMAN

WHAT YOU NEED

Basic Pillows Tool Kit (page 11)

½ yard (45.7 cm) of linen for the pillow front

½ yard (45.7 cm) of checkered cotton for the pillow back

½ yard (45.7 cm) of a solid cotton for the pillow back

½ yard (45.7 cm) of muslin for the pillow form

Paper-backed fusible web

Fabric scraps for the bird appliqués

Black cotton machine-embroidery thread

Appliqué foot (optional)

Water-soluble fabric marker

Darning foot

Orange embroidery floss

Embroidery needle

Thread to match

Button

Polyester fiberfill

SEAM ALLOWANCE

¼ inch (6 mm) unless otherwise noted

FINISHED SIZE

12 x 12 inches (30.5 x 30.5 cm)

What You Cut

Linen
- *1 square, 12½ inches (31.8 cm) square for the pillow front*

Checkered Cotton
- *1 rectangle, 9½ x 12½ inches (24.1 x 31.8 cm) for the pillow back*

Solid Cotton
- *1 rectangle, 9½ x 12½ inches (24.1 x 31.8 cm) for the pillow back*

Muslin
- *2 squares, each 12½ inches (31.8 cm) square for the pillow form*

WHAT YOU DO

1 Trace the templates on page 126. Cut the fabric as described in the box, left. Transfer a reverse image of the traced templates to the paper-backed fusible web. Cut the birds out of the fusible web, leaving a ¼-inch (6 mm) allowance around each shape.

2 Select the fabric scraps you want to use for the birds. Fuse each piece of cut webbing to the wrong side of a fabric scrap. Trim the ¼-inch (6 mm) allowance away.

3 Decide where you want to place the bird appliqués on the linen square. Peel the paper backing off and press to fuse them to the front.

4 Thread your sewing machine with the machine-embroidery thread, and change to an appliqué foot if you have one. Set the machine for a short, straight stitch. Topstitch around the edges of the appliqués. Sew the beaks and feet of the birds at the same time (figure 1). **Note:** You may find it helpful to draw the beaks and feet first using a water-soluble marker.

figure 1

LIGHTEN UP

You can easily change the look of the pillow by using a white fabric for the front and bright fabric scraps for the bird appliqués.

5 Set your machine for free-motion stitching by dropping the feed dogs and changing to the darning foot. Write your text on the pillow front with the soluble marker. Stitch the text in free motion.

6 Thread the embroidery needle with two strands of the orange floss. Fill in just one of the bird's beaks using seed stitches (page 25).

7 Follow the instructions for making an envelope back (page 22). Hem one of the long sides on each of the rectangles cut for the pillow back. Turn the edges under ½ inch (1.3 cm) and press. Turn under again 1 inch (2.5 cm) and press. Make a buttonhole, centering it on the hem of the checkered fabric.

8 Pin the back piece with the buttonhole to the front first—when you turn the pillow you want the buttonhole on top—and sew. Use a zigzag stitch to overcast the seams. Sew on the button.

9 Make the pillow form from the muslin squares (see page 23). Insert the form into your pillow.

MORE THAN YOU KNOW

Recycle men's shirts for the pillow back. You'll be surprised how much fabric you can get out of just one. Thrift stores are a great source for old shirts in vintage fabrics.

twist-n-tie

This interactive cushion is just waiting to play. The threads are left long and knotted on the front side so you can pull them up to adjust the gathers according to your whim. Pull them all tight or leave some loose. Experiment and see what you like best, or change it every day.

WHAT YOU NEED

18-inch (45.7 cm) square of shot silk for the front

2 pieces of shot silk, each 9 x 13 inches (22.9 x 33 cm) for the pillow back

13 inches (33 cm) of cotton fabric for the lining

Machine-embroidery thread to match

12-inch (30.5 cm) square pillow form

SEAM ALLOWANCE

⅝ inch (1.6 cm) unless otherwise noted

FINISHED SIZE

12 x 12 inches (30.5 x 30.5 cm)

DESIGNER

RUTH SINGER

WHAT YOU DO

1 Gather the edges on the square of silk. By hand, fasten a strong thread firmly to one corner of the square. Using small running stitches (page 24), sew a line ¼ inch (6 mm) in from the edge along the side. When you get to the other corner, pull the thread to gather the fabric until the edge measures 13 inches (33 cm) long. Tie off the thread to hold the gathers. Repeat on all sides. You can also machine gather, using long stitches under little tension and pulling the bobbin thread to gather. Press the gathering flat on all sides.

2 To make the ruching, cut a piece of embroidery thread approximately 6 inches (15.2 cm) long. Tie a large knot in one end and stitch a small circle (figure 1). Bring the needle to the front of the fabric to finish, pull up loosely, and knot the thread, leaving at least 2 inches (5.1 cm) of thread hanging loose. Cut off the thread. You should be able to pull the thread tight or leave it fairly loose (figure 2). Repeat five or six times, randomly spacing the ruching over the top of the pillow.

figure 1

figure 2

3 Place the cotton lining right side up on your work surface. Lay the gathered silk square on top of it, right side up, matching the corners and edges. Note: You don't want to catch any of the ruched fabric in the seams when you sew. Pull up on the ruching and pin in place if necessary. Pin around the edges, then machine sew over the gathering. The gathering stitches will be hidden in the seam, but you can remove them if desired.

4 Hem one of the 13-inch (33 cm) edges on each of the back pieces. Turn the edge under ¼ inch (6 mm) and press, then turn under ½ inch (1.3 cm), press, and sew.

5 Follow the instructions for making an envelope back on page 22.

6 Remove any pins used to hold the ruching in place from the pillow front. Insert the pillow form. Pull up or loosen the gathering threads on the ruching as desired.

GIVE IT A SHOT

Though you may not know it by name, shot silk is that yummy iridescent silk that calls to you whenever you pass by the bolt. The shimmer is the result of weaving with two or more different colors. There are synthetic substitutes that offer a nice alternative and lower price. But a pillow uses so little fabric, why not indulge?

tropical blossom

*N*eed a taste of the exotic? This felt flower stays fresh forever. With vibrant shades and layered petals, it'll have you feeling an ocean-kissed tropical breeze in no time. Come on, a girl can dream, right?

DESIGNER

JOAN K. MORRIS

WHAT YOU NEED

Basic Pillows Tool Kit (page 11)

½ yard (45.7 cm) of hot pink felt

⅓ yard (30.2 cm) of orange felt

9 x 12-inch (22.9 x 30.5 cm) piece of purple felt

9 x 12-inch (22.9 x 30.5 cm) piece of yellow felt

2 pieces of green felt, each 9 x 12 inches (22.9 x 30.5 cm)

Thread to match each color

Invisible thread

Polyester fiberfill

Embroidery floss in hot pink

6-inch (15.2 cm) upholstery needle

FINISHED SIZE

13 x 13 inches (33 x 33 cm)

WHAT YOU DO

1 Enlarge the templates on page 122 to use as patterns and cut them out. Make separate bobbins using all the colors of thread. Thread your machine with invisible thread.

2 Fold the piece of hot pink felt in half and pin the large flower pattern to it. Cut a circle around the flower, 1 inch (2.5 cm) out from the edges of the pattern. Using the hot pink bobbin and invisible thread, and **with the paper pattern in place**, machine-stitch as close as you can around all edges of the flower (figure 1). Leave a 4-inch (10.2 cm) opening for stuffing. **Note:** Don't worry if you happen to catch the pattern paper as you stitch—you can easily rip it away later.

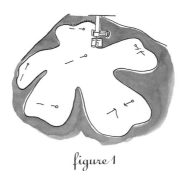

figure 1

3 Using *sharp* scissors, trim the fabric ⅛ inch (3 mm) from the stitching. Be careful not to cut the seam. At the opening, trim as if seamed.

4 Stuff the pillow using a knitting needle or a chopstick to push the stuffing into each petal. Add enough stuffing to make the flower nice and full. Carefully machine-stitch the opening closed.

5 Repeat steps 2–4 for the other flowers, center, and leaves. Cut the medium flower from the orange felt, the small flower from the purple, the center from the yellow, and the leaves from the green. Change bobbin colors accordingly as you sew each piece. Do not stuff these layers as full as the pink flower— you want just enough to give them some padding for quilting.

6 To quilt the orange flower, follow the contour of the petals and stitch around ½ inch (1.3 cm) in from the edge. Then stitch another line, ½ inch (1.3 cm) in from the first.

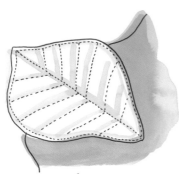

figure 2

7 On the purple flower, stitch once around ½ inch (1.3 cm) in from the edge. On the yellow center, topstitch in from the edge, then stitch across the circle four times creating wedges as for a pie. On the leaves, stitch a center stem and veins sewn on the diagonal (figure 2).

8 Assemble the flower using the hot pink embroidery floss and the upholstery needle. After threading, double the floss and knot. To hide the knot, run the needle from the top center of the hot pink flower through the bottom and back up. Then run the needle up through the orange flower, and then back down through all layers, and back up again. Pull tightly to tuft the pillow. Cut the embroidery floss, leaving a 3-inch (7.6 cm) tail. Tightly pull the floss, tie a knot, and trim the tail.

9 Rethread the needle and knot the floss. Hide the knot by sewing through the top of the orange flower, down through the pink, and back up. Run the thread up through the purple flower, then back down all through layers, and then back up again. Leave a tail, and cut the floss. Tightly tie another knot and trim the tail.

10 Attach the yellow center and make the stamen. Rethread the needle and tie a knot at the end leaving a 1-inch (2.5 cm) tail. Run the floss *down* through the top of the yellow circle so the tail shows, then down through all the layers, and then back up. Leave a tail, cut off the floss, and tie a knot. Trim this tail to 1 inch (2.5 cm) to match the first. Repeat this step two or three more times.

11 Position the leaves on the back of the pink flower, with each sitting between two petals, and pin. Hand-stitch them to the flower using green thread.

child's play

Bring your little artist's sketches to life by transforming them into an embroidered keepsake. Coordinating scraps of patterned fabric and perky rickrack make for a portable gallery you'll want to display in any room in the house.

DESIGNER
CASSI GRIFFIN

WHAT YOU NEED

Basic Pillows Tool Kit (page 11)

3 coordinating scraps of print cotton for fabrics A, B, and C, none less than 4 x 6 inches (10.2 x 15.2 cm)

9 x 18-inch (22.9 x 45.7 cm) piece of print cotton for fabric D

5 x 5-inch (12.7 x 12.7 cm) square of linen for embroidery

Child's drawing to embroider

Water-soluble fabric marker

Embroidery hoop

Embroidery floss

Embroidery needle

1 yard (.9 m) of 1-inch (2.5 cm) rickrack

Polyester fiberfill

SEAM ALLOWANCE

½ inch (1.3 cm) unless otherwise noted

FINISHED SIZE

12 x 4 inches (30.5 x 10.2 cm)

WHAT YOU DO

1 For the front of the pillow, cut 3½ x 5-inch (8.9 x 12.7 cm) rectangles each from fabrics A and D. Take care to cut from the end of fabric D as you will be using the rest of fabric D to create the back of the pillow. Then cut 2½ x 5-inch (6.4 x 12.7 cm) rectangles each from fabrics B and C. Cut another rectangle from fabric D for the back of the pillow that is 5 x 13 inches (12.7 x 33 cm).

2 Transfer the child's drawing to the linen square using the water-soluble fabric marker. Place the fabric in the hoop and embroider using floss colors that coordinate with the fabric prints. Use simple stitches, such as the backstitch, chain stitch, and running stitch (pages 24 and 25). When done, remove the fabric from hoop and press, but do not iron over the embroidery.

3 Piece the cotton prints. Stitch A to B. Then stitch C to the 3½ x 5-inch (8.9 x 12.7 cm) rectangle of fabric D.

4 With right sides together, pin the patch made of fabrics A and B to one side of the embroidered linen square, and pin the patch made from fabrics C and D to the other side (figure 1). Stitch, then press all seams open.

5 Lay the large rectangle cut from fabric D right side up. Following the instructions for sewing rickrack in seams on page 22 (figure 2), pin and baste the rickrack. Pin the pillow front to the back with right sides together. Sew both long ends and one of the short sides.

6 On the open short side, press the seam allowance under at the opening. Trim the corners, then turn pillow right side out. Poke the corners out as needed and press.

7 Stuff with the polyester fiberfill. Do not overstuff. Stitch the opening closed using the slipstitch (page 25).

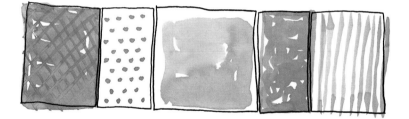

figure 1

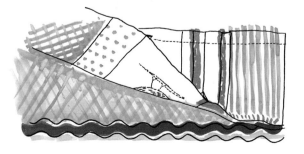

figure 2

smock it

Smocking, a traditional technique for gathering fabric, makes a stylish comeback with these exquisite pillows. Heavily patterned fabric adds another decorative dimension to these not-so-square designs.

DESIGNER
AMANDA HANLEY

WHAT YOU NEED

Basic Pillows Tool Kit (page 11)

1 ½ yards (1.3 m) of cotton or cotton blend fabric

½ yard (45.7 cm) of fusible grid interfacing with 1-inch (2.5 cm) squares

14-inch (35.6 cm) square pillow form

SEAM ALLOWANCE

½ inch (1.3 cm) unless otherwise noted

FINISHED SIZE

14 x 14 inches (35.6 x 35.6 cm)

What You Cut

Cotton Fabric
- *1 square, 26 x 26 inches (66 x 66 cm) for the pillow front*
- *2 rectangles, each 11 x 13 inches (27.9 x 33 cm) for the pillow back*
- *1 square, 13 x 13 inches (33 x 33 cm) for the lining*

Interfacing
- *1 square, 14 x 14 inches (35.6 x 35.6 cm)*

WHAT YOU DO

1 Before cutting, prewash, dry, and iron the fabric. Refer to the stitching guide below. Copy and enlarge it if needed. Cut the fabric as described in the box, left.

2 Center the iron-on interfacing adhesive side down on the wrong side of the pillow front. Follow the manufacturer's instruction to fuse.

3 Thread a needle with approximately 50 inches (1.3 m) of thread, double it, and knot the ends.

4 Following the stitching guide, begin at the starting point by making a small stitch through the grid intersection, then pull tight (figure 1).

figure 1

STITCHING GUIDE

GET ON THE GRID

If you haven't discovered the joys of grid interfacing, now's the time. This iron-on marvel was developed to help quilters stay in line. But creative crafters of all sorts have taken to its straight and narrow ways when they want to accurately align the pieces of their designs.

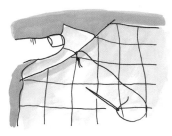

figure 2

5 Next make another small stitch at the grid intersection diagonally up to the left, and pull the thread tight again, bringing the two stitches together and making a fold (figure 2).

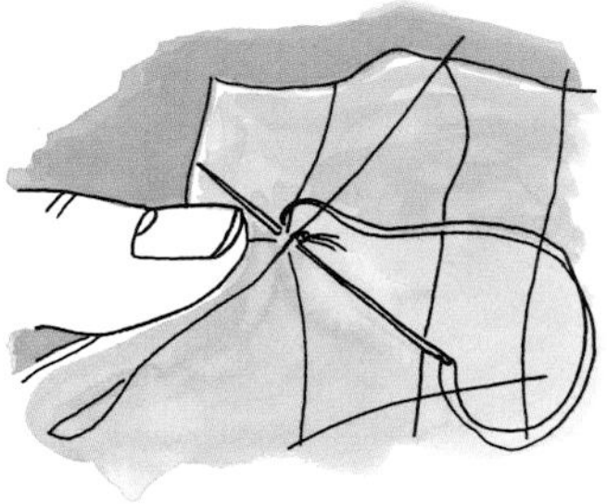

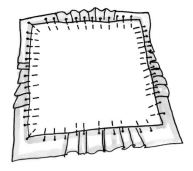

figure 3

6 Make a stitch through these first two stitches and knot together (figure 3).

7 Now make a small stitch through the grid intersection directly below the starting point. *Leave the connecting thread from the previous stitch loose, and knot.* **Note:** A simple way to make these knots as you go is to leave a loop when you first make the stitch, then bring the needle through the loop, and pull tight to make a knot.

8 Repeat steps 4, 5, and 6, stitching diagonally up to the *right.* Repeat step 7.

9 Move down the grid in this fashion until you have completed the first column. Alternate stitching to the left and right as indicated on the stitching guide. If you run out of thread, simply re-thread your needle, knot on top of an existing knot, and finish the column. When you reach the end of a column, rethread your needle, and begin on the next row until all six rows are finished.

10 Flip the fabric over, and *gently* tug and pull the edges to adjust the gathers along the edges.

11 Line the smocked pillow front by placing it right side down on your work surface. Then center the 13-inch (33 cm) square right side down on top of it. Pin the edges on all sides. Flip the pinned piece over so the pillow front is right side up. Pleat the gathers to your liking around all edges (figure 4). Repin the edges as necessary.

figure 4

12 Sew around the edges using a ¼ inch (6 mm) seam allowance. Trim the excess fabric of the pillow front to the edges of the lining to make a square.

13 On each of the pieces cut for the pillow back, turn under ½ inch (1.3 cm) on one of the 13-inch (33 cm) sides and press. Again, fold under ½ inch (1.3 cm), press, and sew using a ⅜-inch (.95 cm) seam allowance. Follow the instructions for making an envelope back on page 22.

Note: Zigzag to overcast the seams before turning. Insert the pillow form.

DIY DOTS

If you can't find grid interfacing, you can use a ruler and triangle to layout the stitch guides on the wrong side of the pillow front. Use a water-soluble fabric marker to space dots at 1-inch (2.5 cm) intervals—12 dots high by 12 dots wide. Be sure to use a marking pen that will not bleed through the fabric.

pretty piecing
&cute quilting

Combine fabulous fabrics
and add terrific quilted textures
for truly stunning results.

two-tone truffles

DESIGNER

AMANDA CARESTIO

$\mathscr{E}$njoy a taste of chocolate now and then? So do we. These delectable pillows feature sweet, little truffle shapes and dark chocolate-dipped color. Yum!

WHAT YOU NEED

Basic Pillows Tool Kit (page 11)

⅜ yd (34.3 cm) of fabric A, a brown print cotton

1 fat quarter of fabric B, an orange print cotton

1 fat quarter of fabric C, a cream cotton

Paper-backed fusible web

Polyester batting

Threads to match

Polyester fiberfill

SEAM ALLOWANCE

½ inch (1.3 cm) unless otherwise noted

FINISHED SIZE

8½ x 11 inches (21.6 x 27.9 cm)

What You Cut

Fabric A
- *3 rectangles, each 9½ x 12 inches (24.1 x 30.5 cm)*
- *1 strip, 3 x 45 inches (7.6 x 114.3 cm). You will need to piece the fabric to make the strip.*

Fabric B
- *1 rectangle, 9½ x 12 inches (24.1 x 30.5 cm)*
- *1 strip, 3 x 45 inches (7.6 x 114.3 cm). You will need to piece the fabric to make the strip.*

Fabric C
- *2 rectangles, each 9½ x 12 inches (24.1 x 30.5 cm)*

Paper-backed fusible web
- *2 rectangles, each 9½ x 12 inches (24.1 x 30.5 cm)*

Batting
- *2 rectangles, each 9½ x 12 inches (24.1 x 30.5 cm)*

WHAT YOU DO

1 You'll make two pillow fronts at one time. Cut the fabric as described in the box, left. Enlarge the pattern on page 123 and transfer it to both pieces of the paper-backed fusible web. Fuse one piece of web to a rectangle cut from fabric A, and the other piece to the rectangle of fabric B.

2 Cut out the motifs and borders following the cutting lines on the pattern. Arrange the pieces on the two rectangles of fabric C. Mix and match colors as desired to pair stalks of fabric A with borders of fabric B or vice versa. Allow a bit of space between elements.

3 Remove the paper backing and fuse the stalks and borders to fabric C. If needed, trim the edges of the borders.

4 Pin each pillow front to a piece of batting. To keep the fabric from shifting as you sew, pin at intervals over the fabric, not just around the edges.

5 Topstitch all edges of the stalks and borders with thread that matches the border color. With the same color thread, machine-quilt the pillow front using stitch lines that follow the contour of the stalks (figure 1). Trim the corners to round them.

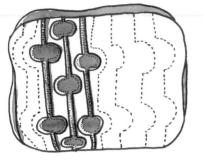

figure 1

6 Attach one strip to the pillow front. Select a strip cut from either fabric A or B, whichever one matches the color of the stalks. Turn under one short end of the strip, press, and stitch. Starting with a stitched end, pin the strip to the front with right sides together and raw edges aligned.

7 Use extra pins to ease the strip around the corners (figure 2). Overlap the starting point. Stitch around the edge of the pillow front. At the point where the strip overlaps, make a line of stitching to sew the strips together.

figure 2

8 Pin the strip to one rectangle of fabric A with right sides together and raw edges aligned. Ease the corners as you did for the pillow front. Stitch, leaving a 5-inch (12.7 cm) opening for turning.

9 Turn the pillow right side out and stuff it. Hand-stitch the opening closed.

10 Using the remaining rectangle of fabric A for the back and the remaining strip for the sides, repeat steps 6–9 to complete the second pillow,

trupunto trio

Why stop at one? Triple your pleasure by making a terrific trio
of trapunto pillows. Once you master the easy technique for
this pillow you'll want to try it again (and again!).
Hint: Stuffing the quilt batting with fiberfill adds the extra loft.

DESIGNER
AMANDA CARESTIO

WHAT YOU NEED

Basic Pillows Tool Kit (page 11)

1 fat quarter of fabric A, a cotton solid in a light color

1 fat quarter of fabric B, a cotton print

1/4 yard (22.8 cm) of fabric C, a cotton solid in a dark color

Polyester quilt batting

Thread to mach

Polyester fiberfill

SEAM ALLOWANCE

1/4 inch (6 mm) unless otherwise noted

FINISHED SIZE

10 1/2 x 9 inches (26.7 x 22.9 cm)

What You Cut

Fabric A
- 1 strip, 2 1/4 x 6 inches (5.7 x 15.2 cm)
- 1 rectangle, 4 1/2 x 6 inches (11.4 x 15.2 cm)

Fabric B
- 2 rectangles, each 3 x 9 inches (7.6 x 22.9 cm)

Fabric C
- 1 strip, 1 1/2 x 6 inches (3.8 x 15.2 cm)
- 1 square, 9 1/2 inches (24.1 cm) square for the back
- 1 rectangle, 4 1/2 x 9 1/2 inches (11.4 x 24.1 cm) for the back

Quilt Batting
- 1 piece, 9 x 10 1/2 inches (22.9 x 26.7 cm)

WHAT YOU DO

1 With right sides together, pin the strip cut from fabric C between the two pieces of fabric A along their 6-inch (15.2 cm) sides. Sew, and then press the seam allowances toward fabric C.

2 With right sides together, stitch the rectangles cut from fabric B to either side of the piece stitched in step 1. Press the seam allowances toward fabric B.

3 Lay the pillow front right side up on the piece of batting. Center the fabric on the batting and pin in place.

4 Using a thread that coordinates with fabric C, topstitch on fabric B 1/8 inch (3 mm) in from the seams.

EASY AS CAN BE

Coordinating a trio of complementary fabrics is easy when you remember a simple rule of three: (1) start with a print or plaid with at least three colors in it; (2) match the light color in the print to a light solid fabric; (3) do the same when choosing a dark solid. It works every time!

5 On fabric A, measure 1 inch (2.5 cm) up from its seam with fabric C. Stitch a horizontal line through both layers that runs across fabric A and between the two pieces of fabric B. From that line of stitching, measure up another 1 inch (2.5 cm) and stitch a line. Continue in this way until you reach the edge of the fabric. You should have a ¼-inch (6 mm) seam allowance left. Do the same, measuring and sewing, from the bottom seam of fabric C.

6 Turn the pillow front over to expose the batting. At the center of each sewn segment, cut one long slit in the batting that runs parallel to the lines of stitching. Make sure you cut only the batting and not the fabric of the pillow front.

7 For the pillow back, hem one edge on the square cut from fabric C. Fold and press the edge under ¼ inch (6 mm). Then fold under again, press, and sew. Follow the instructions on page 22 for making an envelope back. Pin the hemmed square to the pillow front before pinning the un-hemmed rectangle. Do not turn.

8 Stuff the batting for the trapunto effect. Push the polyester fiberfill into the slits you cut in step 6. Fill them to nicely round each segment. Hand-stitch the slits closed.

9 Turn the pillow right side out and stuff with fiberfill. Pin the back opening together, then hand-stitch it closed using the slipstitch (page 25).

10 To round out your trio of pillows, mix and match fabrics by cutting strips and rectangles in different sizes to vary the look of the pieced pillow front. Always remember the batting layer so you can slit and stuff it later.

afternoon tea

DESIGNER
JOAN K. MORRIS

*W*hat says hospitality and comfort more than an invite to tea? This pieced, beaded teapot conveys just the right tone of charm and warmth to any room.

WHAT YOU NEED

Basic Pillows Tool Kit (page 11)

⅛ yard (11.4 cm) each of seven different cotton prints

½ yard (45.7 cm) of white cotton fabric

½ yard (45.7 cm) of a cotton print for the back of the pillow

Paper-backed iron-on adhesive

Thread to match

Invisible thread

Assorted seed beads and E beads to match the fabrics

Beading needle

Polyester fiberfill

SEAM ALLOWANCE

As noted

FINISHED SIZE

14 x 12 inches (35.6 x 30.5 cm)

WHAT YOU DO

1 Enlarge and copy the template on page 122 and cut it out. Carefully cut along the lines as indicated to separate the individual pieces of the teapot: the body, lid, knob, handle, spout, and the hole in the spout.

2 Decide where you want to place each of the seven fabrics on the finished pot and pair them with their pattern piece.

3 Cut the paper-backed iron-on adhesive into pieces large enough to fit the cut-out pattern pieces.

4 Following the manufacturer's instructions, apply the iron-on adhesive to the wrong sides of their corresponding fabrics. Then lay the pattern pieces on the paper backing, trace around them, and cut them out.

5 Cut two 18-inch (45.7 cm) squares from the white cotton fabric. Lay one of them on your work surface. As if putting a puzzle together, lay the pieces of the teapot on it. Make sure to center the design on the square. Starting with the bottom piece of the teapot, remove the paper backing and follow the manufacturer's instructions to adhere. Continue with all pieces until the teapot is assembled.

6 Make a bobbin from the matching thread, and thread the top of your machine with invisible thread. Set your zigzag stitch for a medium width and short length. Zigzag **every** raw edge of the appliquéd fabrics.

7 Bead the fabric. Follow the prints of the different fabrics to guide you in placing the beads. Use the beading needle and invisible thread to sew them on. To keep the beads from falling off in case a thread breaks, knot the thread on the wrong side after sewing every two or three beads.

8 Cut an 18-inch (45.7 cm) square from the fabric for the back of the pillow. Lay it right side up on top of the remaining square of white fabric. Place the beaded pillow top over the layered fabrics with right sides together. Pin through all layers, placing the pins inside the edges of the teapot.

9 Trim in a circle around the teapot, leaving a 1-inch (2.5 cm) allowance around all edges.

10 Set your machine for straight stitching. Sew around the tea pot, using the zigzag stitching around the outer edge as your guide. On the bottom edge, leave a 5-inch (12.7 cm) opening for turning. Trim the seam to ½ inch (1.3 cm), and clip or notch the curves (page 20).

11 Turn right side out. Use a chopstick or knitting needle to push out the handle, lid, and spout. Stuff tightly with fiberfill. Hand-stitch the opening closed.

EXTRA STICKY

Using paper-backed iron-on adhesive gives your fabric extra body. Use it for most craft applications. When you want your fabrics to have a softer hand, use paper-backed fusible web.

logcabin lovely

DESIGNER
KAREN PHILLIPS

Log cabin quilts are very popular, thanks to their simple design and versatility. Ideal for the beginner, the design is worked in strips for an easy play on pattern and color. (And talk about a wonderful excuse to dig up old scraps!)

WHAT YOU NEED

Basic Pillows Tool Kit (page 11)

⅛ yard (11.4 cm) each of cotton for fabric A in a solid, fabric B in a print, fabric C in a polka dot, and fabric D in a floral print

¼ yard (22.8 cm) of a cotton batik print for fabric E and the pillow back

13-inch (33 cm) square of polyester batting

12-inch (30.5 cm) square pillow form

SEAM ALLOWANCE

¼ inch (6 mm) unless otherwise noted

FINISHED SIZE

12 x 12 inches (30.5 x 30.5 cm)

What You Cut

Fabric A
- *2 strips, each 2 x 20 inches (5.1 x 50.8 cm)*

Fabric B
- *1 strip, 2 x 20 inches (5.1 x 50.8 cm)*

Fabric C
- *1 rectangle, 2¼ x 2½ inches (5.7 x 6.4 cm) for the center block*
- *2 strips, each 2 x 20 inches (5.1 x 50.8 cm)*

Fabric D
- *2 strips, each 2 x 20 inches (5.1 x 50.8 cm)*

Fabric E
- *1 rectangle, 1¾ x 2½ inches (4.4 x 6.4 cm) for the center block*
- *3 strips, each 1¼ x 20 inches (3.2 x 50.8 cm)*
- *2 rectangles, each 8 x 12½ inches (20.3 x 31.8 cm) for the pillow back*

WHAT YOU DO

1 Refer to the piecing guide on page 128. Cut the fabric as described in the box, left. The piecing guide is not a template; you will cut your fabric strips to size as you go.

2 For this pillow, you will stitch a center block, then cut and stitch each piece that follows in a spiraling, counter-clockwise direction. Sew the two small rectangles cut from fabric C and E together with right sides facing to make the center block. Press the seam open.

3 Cut a piece from the strip of fabric B to the length of the top of the center block, approximately 3½ inches (8.9 cm). Sew the piece right sides together to the top of the central block. Press the seam open.

figure 1

4 The next piece is cut from a strip of fabric A. From here on it's best to cut the strips as you go. Measure each new strip to the length of the previous sewn strip and cut (figure 1). You can do this using scissors, but using a rotary cutter with a mat is quick and easy, plus you have the benefit of the

mat's grid to guide your cutting line. **Note:** You do not have to add any extra length on the pieces for the seam allowance. All you do is cut, sew, and press.

5 Since you're working in a spiralling counter-clockwise direction, turn the block of sewn fabric one turn to your right before measuring and cutting the next piece. Use the template as your guide. Sew all pieces right sides together and press all seams open.

6 When you've completed piecing the square, pin it right side up to batting, and trim the batting to size.

figure 2

7 Machine-quilt the pillow front to the batting. Start at the center block and spiral around the strips following figure 2. For nice square corners, keep the needle in the fabric when turning.

8 Hem one of the 12½-inch (31.8 cm) sides on each large rectangle cut from fabric E. Turn the edge under ¼ inch (6 mm) and press. Then turn under again, press, and sew. Follow the instructions for making an envelope back on page 22. Insert the pillow form.

NO PROBLEM

The beauty of making a log cabin pillow is that it's okay if your measurements are slightly off or if you sew the strips a bit crooked. This is a great project for using scraps of left-over fabric from other projects; just make sure to coordinate your color scheme by choosing complementary fabrics.

"I do"

*W*hen all the details of the special wedding day
are given such care, why not create a one-of-a-kind keepsake
ring bearer pillow that can be treasured for years to come?
A simple ribbon tie keeps the rings securely in place.

DESIGNER

ELIZABETH HARTMAN

WHAT YOU NEED

Basic Pillows Tool Kit (page 11)

¼ yard (22.8 cm) of silk dupioni

¼ yard (22.8 cm) of a coordinating cotton print

2 blanks for 1-inch (2.5 cm) covered buttons

2 squares of lightweight fusible interfacing, 9 x 9 inches (22.9 x 22.9 cm)

Polyester fiberfill

Water-soluble fabric marker

Embroidery floss

1 yard (.9 m) of ⅜-inch (9.5 mm) organdy ribbon

FOR THE OPTIONAL APPLIQUÉ

5-inch (12.7 cm) square of white wool felt

5-inch (12.7 cm) square of paper-backed fusible web

Thread to match

Black embroidery floss (optional)

SEAM ALLOWANCE

½ inch (1.3 cm) unless otherwise noted

FINISHED SIZE

9 x 9 inches (22.9 x 22.9 cm)

What You Cut

Silk Dupioni

- *1 square, 4 x 4 inches (10.2 x 10.2 cm)*
- *2 strips, each 1 ½ x 4 inches (3.8 x 10.2 cm)*
- *2 strips, each 1 ½ x 6 inches (3.8 x 15.2 cm)*
- *2 strips, each 2 x 6 inches (5.1 x 15.2 cm)*
- *2 strips, each 2 x 9 inches (5.1 x 22.9 cm)*

Cotton Print

- *Cut exactly the same as for the silk dupioni*

WHAT YOU DO

1 Cut the fabric as described in the box, above. Following the manufacturer's instructions, use scraps of the silk and cotton to cover the two button blanks, one in each fabric.

2 Follow figure 1 to piece the back of the pillow first. Placing right sides together, and using a ¼-inch (6 mm) seam allowance, sew one of the 1½ x 4-inch (3.8 x 10.2 cm) silk strips to the top and one to the bottom of the 4-inch (10.2 cm) cotton square. Press the seams open.

3 Sew the two 1½ x 6-inch (3.8 x 15.2 cm) silk strips to the left and right sides of the square, creating a frame around it. Repeat the same process by sewing the two 2 x 6-inch (5.1 x 15.2 cm) strips of printed cotton to the top and bottom of the block and the two 2 x 9-inch (5.1 x 22.9 cm) strips to the left and right sides.

4 Press all seams open. Fuse one of the squares of fusible interfacing to the wrong side of the pieced block.

figure 1

5 Make the front of the pillow by repeating steps 2–4. Your center square will be silk framed in printed cotton with an exterior frame of silk, as shown in figure 1.

6 With right sides together, stitch the front and back pillow panels together, leaving a 3-inch (7.6 cm) opening on one of the sides for turning.

7 Trim the corners and turn the pillow right side out. Push out the corners if needed. Use the fiberfill to stuff the pillow to the desired fullness, and hand-stitch the opening closed.

8 Use a ruler and soluble marker to lightly mark the center point of both the front and back of the pillow. Thread a long sewing needle with approximately 18 inches (45.7 cm) of embroidery floss. Using the covered buttons, follow the instructions on page 23 for tufting a pillow.

9 Tie the organdy ribbon around the silk-covered button on the pillow's front and trim as desired.

OPTIONAL APPLIQUÉ

1 After completing step 5 for the pillow, copy the template on page 127 and cut it out. Use it to trace the shape onto the paper side of the fusible web. Press to fuse the web to the wrong side of the felt. Allow to cool and cut out the bird.

2 Remove the paper and position the appliqué in the top left corner of the front pillow panel, with its beak approximately 1 ½ inches (3.8 cm) from the center of the pillow. You want the bird to appear as if it's carrying the ribbon with the rings. Once you're satisfied with the appliqué's location, cover the area with a scrap cloth or lightweight towel and press it in place.

3 Use the zigzag, satin, or buttonhole stitch on your machine to carefully sew around the edges of the appliqué. If desired, use the black embroidery floss to stitch an eye on the bird. Then finish the pillow as above.

spot on

*I*f you're the type who just can't decide on one fabric, you'll enjoy this project that puts a happy dozen in the spotlight. Circular designs, spiraling surface stitches, and an easy grid pattern bring everything together.

DESIGNER

MALKA DUBRAWSKY

WHAT YOU NEED

Basic Pillows Tool Kit (page 11)

12 fabric scraps of print cotton, none less than 4 inches (10.2 cm) square

⅜ yard (34.3 cm) of print cotton for the pillow back

4-inch (10.2 cm) fabric squares for the appliqués: 5 of unbleached muslin, 4 of bleached cotton, 2 in ecru cotton, 1 in pale blue cotton

14-inch (35.6 cm) square of muslin for quilting

14-inch (35.6) square of cotton batting

2 strips of print cotton, 1¼ x 28 inches (3.2 x 71.1 cm) for the binding

2 pieces of muslin, each 9½ x 12½ inches (24.1 x 31.8 cm) for the pillow form

Safety pins

12-inch (30.5 cm) zipper

Darning foot

Zipper foot

Polyester fiberfill

SEAM ALLOWANCE

¼ inch (6 mm) unless otherwise noted

FINISHED SIZE

13 x 10 inches (33 x 25.4 cm)

WHAT YOU DO

1 Copy the template on page 127 and cut it out. Use it to trace 12 circles, one on each of the different fabric scraps. Cut them out. Cut two pieces for the pillow back from the print cotton, each 14 x 12 inches (35.6 x 30.5 cm) and set aside.

2 Machine-stitch ¼ inch (6 mm) in from the edge around each circle cut in step 1. Clip the seam, spacing the cuts approximately ¼ inch (6 mm) apart. Be careful to avoid cutting the stitching. On the wrong side, press the clipped edge toward the middle of the circle (figure 1).

figure 1

3 Center, and then pin a circle right side up on each of the 4-inch (10.2 cm) fabric squares. Edgestitch each circle to its square.

4 Arrange the squares in a pleasing manner to make a rectangle with three squares down and four across. Pin the first line of three squares to each other making a strip. Sew, and press the seams either to the right or left. Repeat to make another strip. Pin and sew the two strips together along their long edges and press.

5 Repeat step 4 to make another set of sewn strips. Sew the two sets together to complete the pieced top.

6 Lay the 14-inch (35.6 cm) square of muslin on your work surface. Lay the 14-inch (35.6 cm) square of batting on top of it. Lay the pieced top right side up on both layers of fabric and pin with safety pins thorough all layers.

7 With white thread, and using the darning foot on your sewing machine, sew through all layers to quilt. Use free-motion quilting to make concentric circles on each of the appliquéd circles. Trim the edges of the layers flush.

8 On one of the long edges of one piece of fabric cut for the back, turn under ¼ inch (6 mm) and press. Turn under again 1½ inches (3.8 cm) and press. On one of the long edges of the other back piece, turn under ¼ inch (6 mm) and press. Follow the instructions for making a zippered back on page 23.

9 Sew the strips for the binding together to make one long strip as for making bias tape on page 21.

10 Bind the edges and miter the corners following the instructions on page 21. Before you begin sewing the binding to the raw edge, leave a 4-inch (10.2 cm) tail for overlapping. Once you turn the binding over the raw edge, use a zigzag stitch to hold it down.

11 Using the two pieces of muslin, make the pillow form following the instructions on page 23. Insert the form into the pillow.

WHY CUT?

Save time by using the precut squares of cotton favored by quilters. They're sold in blocks and grouped by fabric type and/or colorways. But be careful. They're so cute you may be tempted to buy way more than you need.

new neutral

A strategically off-center focal point, delicate surface detailing, and a thoroughly modern aesthetic make this quilted work of art an elegant accent to any room. Trés chic!

DESIGNER

MALKA DUBRAWSKY

WHAT YOU NEED

Basic Pillows Tool Kit (page 11)

7 fabric scraps of print cotton in pale shades and white, none less than 4 x 10 inches (10.2 x 25.4 cm)

¼ yard (22.8 cm) of bleached cotton

¼ yard (22.8 cm) of unbleached cotton muslin

½ yard (45.7 cm) of print cotton for the pillow back

⅛ yard (11.4 cm) of print cotton for the binding

18-inch (45.7 cm) square of cotton muslin for quilting

18-inch (45.7 cm) square of cotton batting

Safety pins

Darning foot

12-inch (30.5 cm) zipper

Zipper foot

12 x 12-inch (30.5 x 30.5 cm) pillow form

SEAM ALLOWANCE

¼ inch (6 mm) unless otherwise noted

FINISHED SIZE

13 x 13 inches (33 x 33 cm)

WHAT YOU DO

1 Copy and enlarge the template on page 125 and cut out the pieces.

2 Pin pieces 1–7 of the template to the seven different print cotton scraps and cut them out. Pin pieces 8, 12, 13, 14, and 17 to the bleached white cotton and cut. Pin pieces 9, 11, 15, and 16 to the unbleached cotton muslin and cut.

3 Cut two pieces, each 9 x 18 inches (22.9 x 45.7 cm), from the fabric for the pillow back. Cut the fabric for the binding on the diagonal into strips that are 1¼ inches (3.2 cm) wide.

4 Make the pillow top. Using the template as reference, sew piece 1 to piece 2 along the edge as noted, and press. Sew piece 3 to the two stitched pieces and press. Continue sewing the pieces of the pillow top in order, pressing them as you go.

5 Lay the 18-inch (45.7 cm) square of muslin on your work surface. Lay the 18-inch (45.7 cm) square of batting on top and the pieced top right side up on both layers of fabric. Pin with safety pins through all layers.

figure 1

6 With white thread, and using the darning foot on your sewing machine, quilt the layers. Use free-motion quilting to make a diamond pattern (figure 1). Remove the pins as you sew. Trim the edges of the layers flush.

7 On one of the long edges of one piece of fabric cut for the back, turn under ¼ inch (6 mm) and press. Turn under again 1½ inches (3.8 cm) and press. On one of the long edges of the other back piece, turn under ¼ inch (6 mm) and press. Follow the instructions for making a zippered back on page 23.

8 Lay the quilted pillow front on the zippered back with wrong sides together and pin. Trim the pieces flush. Sew the front to the back around the edges.

9 Sew the strips for the binding together to make one long strip as for making bias tape on page 21.

10 Bind the edges and miter the corners following the instructions on page 21. Before you begin sewing the binding to the raw edge, leave a 4-inch (10.2 cm) tail for overlapping. Once you turn the binding over the raw edge, use a zigzag stitch to hold it down.

11 Stuff the pillow with the form.

cathedralwindows

DESIGNER

TIFFANY ANN NELSON

This perennial favorite gets a fresh update with brightly colored batik fabric contrasted with crisp, white cotton. This project will demand some patience on your part, but you will be well-rewarded with a classic object of real beauty.

WHAT YOU NEED

Basic Pillows Tool Kit (page 11)

½ yard (45.7 cm) of white cotton

⅓ yard (30.2 cm) of cotton batik fabric for the pillow back

Fabric scraps of batik fabric in four to 12 different patterns

White thread

12-inch (30.5 cm) square pillow form

SEAM ALLOWANCE

¼ inch (6 mm) unless otherwise noted

FINISHED SIZE

11½ x 11½ inches (29.2 x 29.2 cm)

What You Cut

White Cotton
• 9 squares, each 8½ inches (21.6 cm) square for the pillow front

Batik Fabric
• 2 rectangles, each 11½ x 15 inches (29.2 x 38.1 cm) for the pillow back

Batik Fabric Scraps
• 12 squares, each 2¼ inches (5.7 cm) square for the pillow front

---

WHAT YOU DO

1 Cut the fabric as described in the box, left. With the right side up, fold the edges of an 8½-inch (21.6 cm) square in toward the center ¼ inch (6 mm) and press. This will be the right side of the square. Now find the center of the square by first folding it in half lengthwise with right sides together, and then lightly pressing the fold. Unfold the square, fold it widthwise, and press. The center is where the fold lines cross.

2 Bring each corner of the square to the center and press (figure 1).

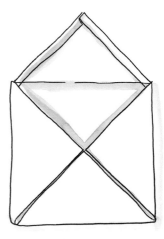

figure 1

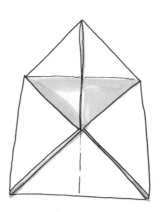

figure 2

3 Once again, bring each corner to the center and press (figure 2). You should now have a folded 4-inch (11.4 cm) square. Repeat steps 1–3 on the remaining white-cotton squares.

4 Thread a needle with white thread and knot one end. Sew up from the center back of a folded square. Tack the four corners where they meet in the center on the middle layer first, then tack the four corners where they meet in the center on the top layer. Bring the thread back down through the bottom of the square, finish off, and cut the thread.

5 Take two of the folded squares and place them side by side with right sides up. Using the whipstitch (page 25) sew the squares together along one side and finish off. Add another square and sew to make a strip with three squares across. Repeat this step two more times until you have three strips of three squares each. Next, sew one strip to another strip along one of the long sides, then sew the remaining strip to them. When finished, you will have nine squares sewn together to make a piece three squares across and three squares down.

6 Turn one of the 2¼-inch (5.1 cm) batik squares to look like a diamond, and lay it on the seam between the first and second square in the top row. Pin the batik square in the middle to anchor it while you stitch around it.

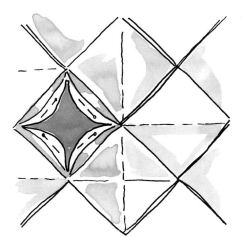

figure 3

7 Pull back the top layer of folds and lay it over the square approximately ¼ inch (6 mm) and pin in place on all four sides, as shown in figure 3. With a needle and thread, slipstitch (page 25) the folded white cotton down over the batik square on all four sides. Repeat eleven more times, placing the different batik patterns randomly as you please. Alternate the number of batik squares in each row, two in the first and third rows, and three in second and fourth.

8 For the pillow back, hem one of the short sides on each of the 11½ x 15-inch (29.2 x 38.1 cm) batik rectangles. Turn the edge under ¼ inch (6 mm) and press, then turn under again ½ inch (1.3 cm) and press. Sew the hem ¼ inch (6 mm) in from the fold. Follow the instructions for making an envelope back on page 22. The finished size of the pillow will be an 11½-inch (29.2 cm) square. When you insert the pillow form, it should plump up nicely.

surprising spins

Turn your notion of a pillow
on its head with these creative
interpretations of the form.

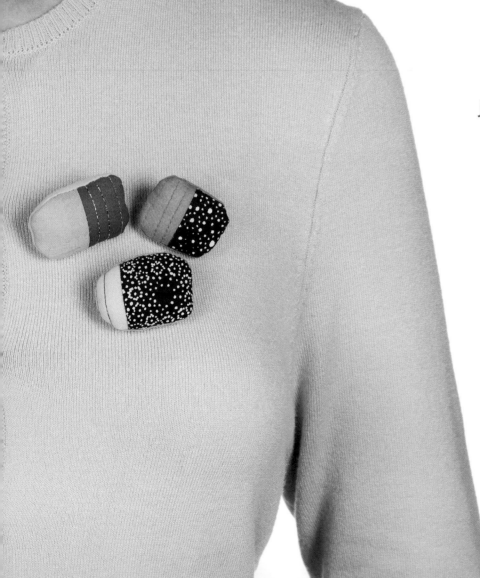

bonbon brooches

DESIGNER

JENNIFER COOKE

*P*illows don't just comfort your body—they can decorate it, too. Make a bold fashion statement with these scrap-busting brooches in eye-catching colors and contrasting thread.

WHAT YOU NEED

Basic Pillows Tool Kit (page 11)

Cotton fabric scraps

Batting scraps

Thread to match or contrast

Metallic thread (optional)

Tailor's chalk or water-soluble fabric marker

Polyester fiberfill

Metal pin back

SEAM ALLOWANCE

¼ inch (6 mm) unless otherwise noted

FINISHED SIZE

1 x 1½ inches (2.5 x 3.8 cm)

WHAT YOU DO

1 Copy the template on page 127 and cut it out. For the front of the pin, cut 2-inch (5.1 cm) squares from two different fabric scraps. For the back of the pin, cut two strips from the same solid-color fabric scrap, one 2 x 4 inches (5.1 x 10.2 cm) and one 2½ x 4 inches (6.4 x 10.2 cm). You'll trim these strips later, so you don't need to be exact when cutting.

2 Stitch the two front pieces together along one edge. Press the seams to one side, either right or left.

3 Cut the quilt batting to the same size as the stitched front. Lay the front right side up on top of the batting. Sew straight lines, approximately ⅛ inch (3 mm) apart, to quilt the top.

4 For the back of the pin, fold one of the long edges on the wider strip under ¼ inch (6 mm) and press. With right sides up, overlap the raw edge on the narrower strip with the folded edge on the other strip and pin.

ONE OF A KIND

Experiment by creating your own pin template to alter the shape. For even more fun, quilt the top using free-form machine stitching—just drop the presser foot to swirl and twirl the fabric at will.

5 With right sides facing, lay the front of the pin on the back. Center the template on the fabric, and trace around it using tailor's chalk or a water-soluble fabric marker.

6 Using the traced line as your stitching guide, sew through all layers of fabric. Backstitch as you complete the oval. Trim the seam. Clip the curves carefully—take small snips!

7 Turn the pin right side out through the opening on the back and press. Stuff the pillow with the fiberfill. A tapestry needle or chopstick is helpful for stuffing small items.

8 Hand-stitch the back of the pin closed along the folded edge. Center the metal pin back on the seam and sew it to the back.

A LITTLE BLING

Use metallic thread for the decorative stitching. Since it has a tendency to break under tension, only use the metallic thread for the bobbin. Thread the top of the machine with a matching color of regular thread and stitch with the wrong side up. The shiny metallic will appear on the front of your pin.

fabulous foldout

WHAT YOU NEED

Basic Pillows Tool Kit (page 11)

½ yard (45.7 cm) of a striped fabric

½ yard (45.7 cm) of microfiber

12 x 13-inch (30.5 x 38.1 cm) piece of 1-inch (2.5 cm) foam

3 x 22-inch (7.6 x 55.9 cm) strip of faux leather

20 inches (50.8 cm) of 5 mm piping cord

12 inches (30.5 cm) of thick black elastic cord

Embroidery floss

Embroidery needle

1 large decorative button

Zipper foot

SEAM ALLOWANCE

½ inch (1.3 cm) unless otherwise noted

FINISHED SIZE

13 x 6¾ inches (33 x 17.1 cm)

Here's a little something extra to cheer about at the next game. Use your team's colors for this handy folding cushion, and you'll be a hit in the stands all season long.

DESIGNER

JOAN K. MORRIS

What You Cut

Striped Fabric

- 1 rectangle, 15 x 16 inches (38.1 x 40.6 cm) with stripes running parallel to the length

Microfiber

- 1 rectangle, 13 x 14 inches (33 x 35.6 cm)

WHAT YOU DO

1 Cut the fabric as described in the box, left. To shape the corners of the pillow, center the striped fabric, right side down, over the piece of foam. The fabric will drape over the sides. At the corners, pinch and pin the fabric together (figure 1). Machine-stitch where you pinned. Trim the excess.

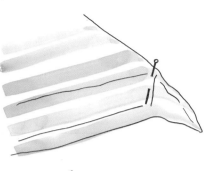

figure 1

2 Make the handles. Cut both the strip of faux leather and length of 5 mm piping cord in half.

3 Place one piece of piping cord lengthwise in the center of one of the strips of faux leather. With the zipper foot on the sewing machine, stitch as close as you can to the piping cord.

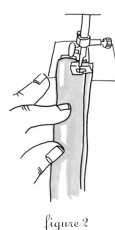

figure 2

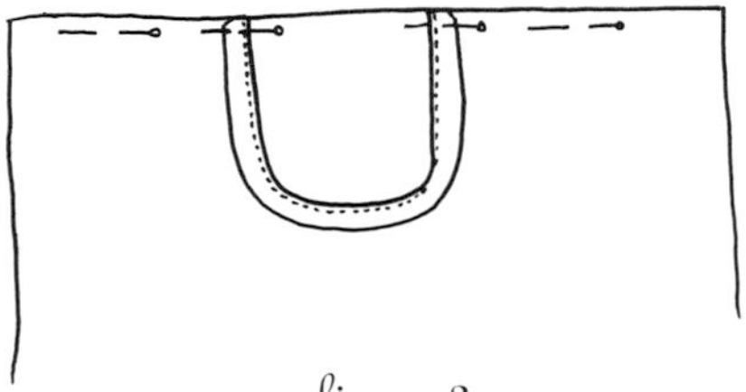

figure 3

4 Trim one side of the seam allowance to ⅛ inch (3 mm), leaving the other side long. Fold the longer side over the trimmed side, turn the raw edge under, and hand-stitch in place (figure 2). Repeat steps 3 and 4 to make the other handle.

5 With the piece of microfiber right side up, pin one of the handles to one of the short ends of the fabric. Position it 3 inches (7.6 cm) in from both the sides. Align the raw ends of the handle with the raw edge of the fabric, pin, and baste in place (figure 3). Attach the other handle to the striped fabric in the same way.

6 Fold the piece of black elastic cord in half, making a loop at one end. Position the elastic in between the two ends of the handle sewn to the microfiber. As you did for the handle, align the raw ends of the elastic with the raw edges of the fabric, pin, and baste.

7 Lay the microfiber piece right side up on your work surface and lay the foam on top of it. Lay the striped fabric right side down on the foam. Pin the fabrics together along three edges: both of the ends with the handles, and one of the longer sides. Make sure the handles and elastic are free of the seam. Pin carefully at the corners.

8 Pull the foam out, and machine-stitch around the three pinned edges. Turn the piece right side out and push out the corners. Slide the foam back inside. Turn the raw edge on the striped fabric under and hand-stitch it to the microfiber to close the side.

9 Fold the pillow in half with the striped fabric to the inside. Pull the elastic loop through the handles to the other side to help you decide where to place the button. Use the embroidery floss and needle to attach the button.

woodland keychains

DESIGNER

AIMEE RAY

Never misplace your keys again with these adorable sculptural forms.
Just attach to readily available metal keychain loops
for irresistibly cute accessories that make great quick gifts.

WHAT YOU NEED

Basic Pillows Tool Kit (page 11)

9 x 12-inch (22.9 x 30.5 cm) pieces of felt, one each in cream, tan, light brown, dark brown, and red

Thread to match

Embroidery floss in cream and brown

Polyester fiberfill

3 keychain rings

FINISHED SIZE

2 x 2 inches (5.1 x 5.1 cm)

WHAT YOU DO

1 Copy and cut out the templates on page 129. Cut around the outermost edges.

2 Trace the shapes on the felt: cream for the squirrel and acorn; tan for the mushroom. Cut two of each.

3 Trim the templates. Follow the lines to separate the individual pieces. Use these pieces to trace the shapes onto the colors of felt as shown on the templates, then cut the pieces out.

4 Pin each felt piece in place on top of *one* of its corresponding background pieces. Stitch them on with matching thread or one strand of embroidery floss, using tiny straight stitches around the edges.

5 Embroider the shapes. Using cream floss and the satin stitch (page 25), embroider the spots on the mushroom. Using brown floss and the satin stitch, embroider the eye and nose on the squirrel. Using brown floss and the split stitch (page 25), embroider the lines on the squirrel's tail and on the acorn.

6 Pin the front and back pieces of each shape wrong sides together, and sew along the edges using the whipstitch (page 25). Before closing them up, stuff with a bit of fiberfill.

7 Sew a keychain ring to the top of each pillow using embroidery floss.

quick change

DESIGNER
JOAN K. MORRIS

*P*resto chango! When you want to change this pillow, simply unhook the elastic, reverse the flaps by turning them to the other side of the pillow, and hook them to the button on the other side.

WHAT YOU NEED

Basic Pillows Tool Kit (page 11)

½ yard (45.7 cm) of fabric A, a light print for the pillow back

½ yard (45.7 cm) of fabric B, a dark print for the pillow top
¼ yard (22.8 cm) each of four different light cotton prints

¼ yard (22.8 cm) each of four different dark cotton prints

1 package of 1-inch (2.5 cm) piping

20 inches (50.8 cm) of 2 mm black elastic cord

½ yard (45.7 cm) of batting

Polyester fiberfill

2 black ¾-inch (1.9 cm) shank buttons

Black embroidery floss

Embroidery needle

Zipper foot

SEAM ALLOWANCE

½ inch (1.3 cm) unless otherwise noted

FINISHED SIZE

12 x 12 inches (30.5 x 30.5 cm)

WHAT YOU DO

1 Enlarge the template on page 122 and cut it out. Use it to cut out eight triangles, one each from the four light cotton prints, and one each from the four dark cotton prints. Pair the triangles, one light with one dark. These will become the reversible flaps of the pillow.

2 Cut a 13-inch (33 cm) square, one each from fabric A and fabric B.

3 Cut four pieces of piping, each 20 inches (50.8 cm) long. Cut four pieces of the black elastic cord, each 5 inches (12.7 cm) long.

4 With raw edges aligned and right sides up, pin a piece of piping around the two short sides of one triangle of a pair. Stitch the piping to the triangle using the zipper foot on your machine.

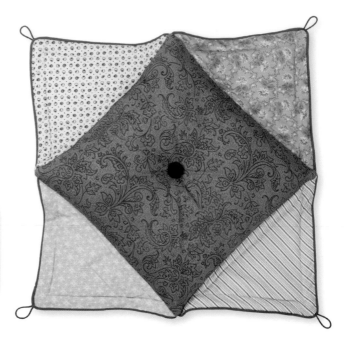

FEEL GOOD

For a truly dynamic look and feel, consider using fabrics with different textures on each flap. For example, try: flannel, linen, wool, or fleece.

5 Fold one of the elastic pieces in half. Lay the elastic on the piping at the tip of the triangle, aligning the raw ends of the elastic with the raw edges of the seam allowance (figure 1). The loop of elastic will be pointing to the base of the triangle. Pin and sew.

figure 1

6 Lay the other triangle from the pair on its mate, right sides together. Pin along the edges with the piping. With the zipper foot on your sewing machine, stitch them together. Turn right side out, and press flat. Repeat steps 4–6 on the remaining pairs of triangles.

7 Cut four triangles out of the batting. As these triangles need to be shorter than the fabric triangles, trim 1 inch (2.5 cm) off the base of the triangle pattern before cutting.

8 Lay one batting triangle inside each flap, push it snug into the point, and pin in place. Topstitch the triangles ¾ inch (1.9 cm) in from the edges all the way around.

9 Lay the square of fabric A right side up on your work surface. Lay the flaps with dark sides down on top of the square. Align the raw edges. The tip of each triangle with the elastic loop should be pointing toward the center of the square. Use a ¼-inch (6 mm) seam allowance around all edges to baste in place.

10 Place the square of fabric B on top of the square of fabric A with flaps right sides together. Pin through all layers. Machine-stitch around the edges, leaving a 5-inch (12.7 cm) opening for turning. Trim the corners (page 19) and turn the piece right side out.

11 Use the fiberfill to stuff the pillow. Turn the edges of the opening under, and stitch closed.

12 Follow the instructions for tufting on page 23 using the embroidery needle and the black embroidery floss to attach the buttons.

13 Hook the elastic loops around the button.

restful moment

DESIGNER

NATHALIE MORNU

WHAT YOU NEED

Basic Pillows Tool Kit (page 11)

⅛ yard (11.4 cm) of printed fabric for the front

⅛ yard (11.4 cm) of solid charmeuse for the back

¼ yard (22.8 cm) of striped cotton for the piping

1 yard (.9 m) of piping cord

8 x 5-inch (20.3 x 12.7 cm) scrap of batting

1 yard (.9 m) of narrow ribbon

Zipper foot

SEAM ALLOWANCE

½ inch (1.3 cm) unless otherwise noted

FINISHED SIZE

7½ x 3½ inches (19 x 8.9 cm)

*D*o you ever wish you could pause time and take a break from it all? Close your eyes and rest without a care in the world? We can't promise utopia, but we do think this gentle eye pillow will get you a little bit closer with its soothing fabric and do-not-disturb ribbon ties.

WHAT YOU DO

1 Enlarge the pattern pieces on page 127 and cut them out. Cut out the fabric pieces.

2 Hem the straight ends of both back pieces by turning them under ½ inch (1.3 cm), then under again ½ inch (1.3 cm), and stitching.

3 Place the back right piece right side up. Put the back left over it, also right side up, so its hemmed edge overlaps the hem of the back right by ½ inch (1.3 cm). Pin the pieces together and baste along the upper and lower center edges (figure 1). Set aside.

4 Using the piping fabric, cut four strips on the bias 1¾ inches (4.4 cm) wide, and stitch them together to make bias tape (page 21). Place the piping cord lengthwise in the center of the bias strip. With the zipper foot on the sewing machine, stitch as close as you can to the piping cord. Trim the seam to ½ inch (1.3 cm) and clip it every ½ inch (1.3 cm).

5 Pin the piping to the right side of the pieces you basted together in step 3, matching the raw edges. Turn under one of the piping ends and overlap the other end so they won't show later. Baste around the exterior of the piping (figure 2).

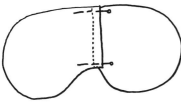

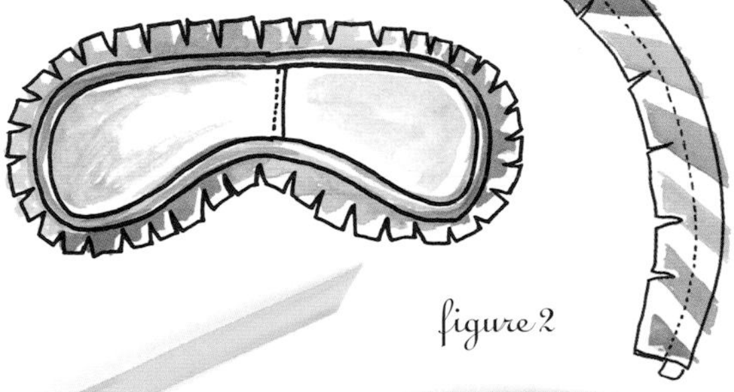

figure 1

figure 2

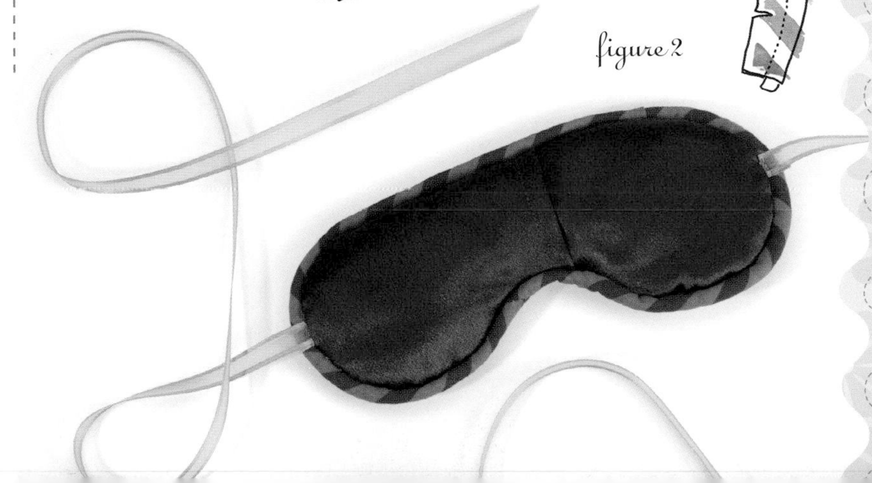

6 Pin the front on the back, right sides together and matching raw edges. Baste all around, sewing to the exterior of the piping.

7 Machine-stitch all around. Clip and notch the seams, then turn right side out.

8 Using the pattern piece for the front as a template, cut out the batting, then slip it inside the eye pillow. Cut two lengths of ribbon, each 15 inches (38.1 cm) long. Hand-stitch the ribbon on either side to make ties.

SOOTHING TIPS

If you're an aromatherapy buff, instead of inserting a piece of batting inside the eye pillow, fill it with a dried herb such as lavender. Flaxseed is a nice alternative as well. Rather than putting these directly inside, make a little case shaped a bit smaller than the eye pillow. Fill it with the herbs or seeds, stitch it shut, and tuck it inside the eye pillow. You can then chill the pillow in the fridge or pop it in the microwave to heat it up, depending on the type of soothing you seek.

sweet tooth

Who among us doesn't recall the anticipation of a nighttime visit from the Tooth Fairy? Carry on an honored tradition with this candy-colored pocket pillow, ready to hang from the door.

DESIGNER

NATHALIE MORNU

WHAT YOU NEED

Basic Pillows Tool Kit (page 11)

¼ yard (22.8 cm) of fabric for the pocket

¼ yard (22.8 cm) of fabric for the body of the pillow

Water-soluble marker

Embroidery hoop

Embroidery floss

Embroidery needle

1 yard (.9 m) of ribbon, ³/₁₆ inch (5 mm) wide

Polyester fiberfill

SEAM ALLOWANCE

½ inch (1.3 cm) unless otherwise noted

FINISHED SIZE

9½ x 5½ inches (24.1 x 14 cm)

WHAT YOU DO

1 Enlarge the templates on page 123 and cut them out.

2 Trace the outline of the pocket template onto the appropriate fabric but **don't** cut it out. Transfer the embroidery design onto the fabric, and write your child's name nearby with the soluble marker, making sure to stay within ½ inch (1.3 cm) of the inside of the outline to accommodate the seam allowance.

3 Using the embroidery hoop to hold the fabric, embroider the designs using the floss and the embroidery needle. Use the outline or stem stitch (page 24) for the design and name, and make French knots (page 24) for the eyes.

4 Cut the pocket. Fold it with wrong sides together at the fold line and press. Cut a piece of ribbon 7¼ inches (18.4 cm) long. On the embroidered half of the pocket, pin the ribbon close to the edge of the fold (figure 1), and stitch it down. Trim away the excess ribbon at either end.

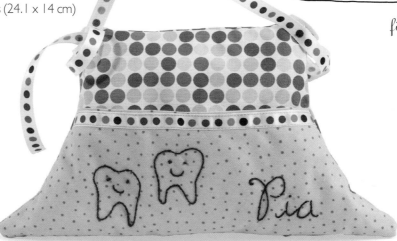

figure 1

5 Cut the pieces for the body of the pillow out of the fabric. Place one right side up on your work surface. Lay the pocket with embroidered side up over it, matching raw edges. Over these, lay the second body piece, right side down with raw edges aligned. Pin, and then stitch, leaving a 4-inch (10.2 cm) opening along the bottom edge. Clip the corners and curves, and turn right side out.

6 Stuff the pillow lightly. Slip-stitch (page 25) the opening closed.

7 Hand-sew the remaining ribbon to the upper corners of the pillow to make a handle for hanging. For a whimsical touch, loop the ribbon at the corners then secure the loops with a tiny knot.

marvelous muff

Kiss cold fingers goodbye, and
say hello to fashion. You'll be fabulous
(and warm) in faux fur, whether on
the town or lounging on the couch!

DESIGNER

JOAN K. MORRIS

WHAT YOU NEED

Basic Pillows Tool Kit (page 11)

12 x 15-inch (30.5 x 38.1 cm) piece of 1-inch (2.5 cm) foam

½ yard (45.7 cm) of brocade

½ yard (45.7 cm) of white faux fur

1¼ yard (1.1 m) of 1-inch (2.5 cm) brocade ribbon

White thread

Invisible thread

White embroidery floss

Embroidery needle

SEAM ALLOWANCE

½ inch (1.3 cm) unless otherwise noted

FINISHED SIZE

13 x 7½ inches (33 x 19 cm)

What You Cut

Brocade
- 1 piece, 15 x 17 inches (38.1 x 43.2 cm)

Faux Fur
- 2 strips, each 3 x 17 inches (7.6 x 43.2 cm)
- 1 piece, 15 x 17 inches (38.1 x 43.2 cm)

WHAT YOU DO

1 Pin the two strips of faux fur on either long side of the brocade, aligning the raw edges. Make a bobbin using the white thread, and thread the top of your machine with the invisible thread. Use a zigzag stitch to machine-baste the fur to the brocade.

2 Cut the length of ribbon in half. Lay the pieces of ribbon, half on the fur, half on the brocade fabric, over each basted seam (figure 1). Machine-stitch the ribbon to the fabric along each long edge, stitching as close to the edge of the ribbon as possible.

figure 1

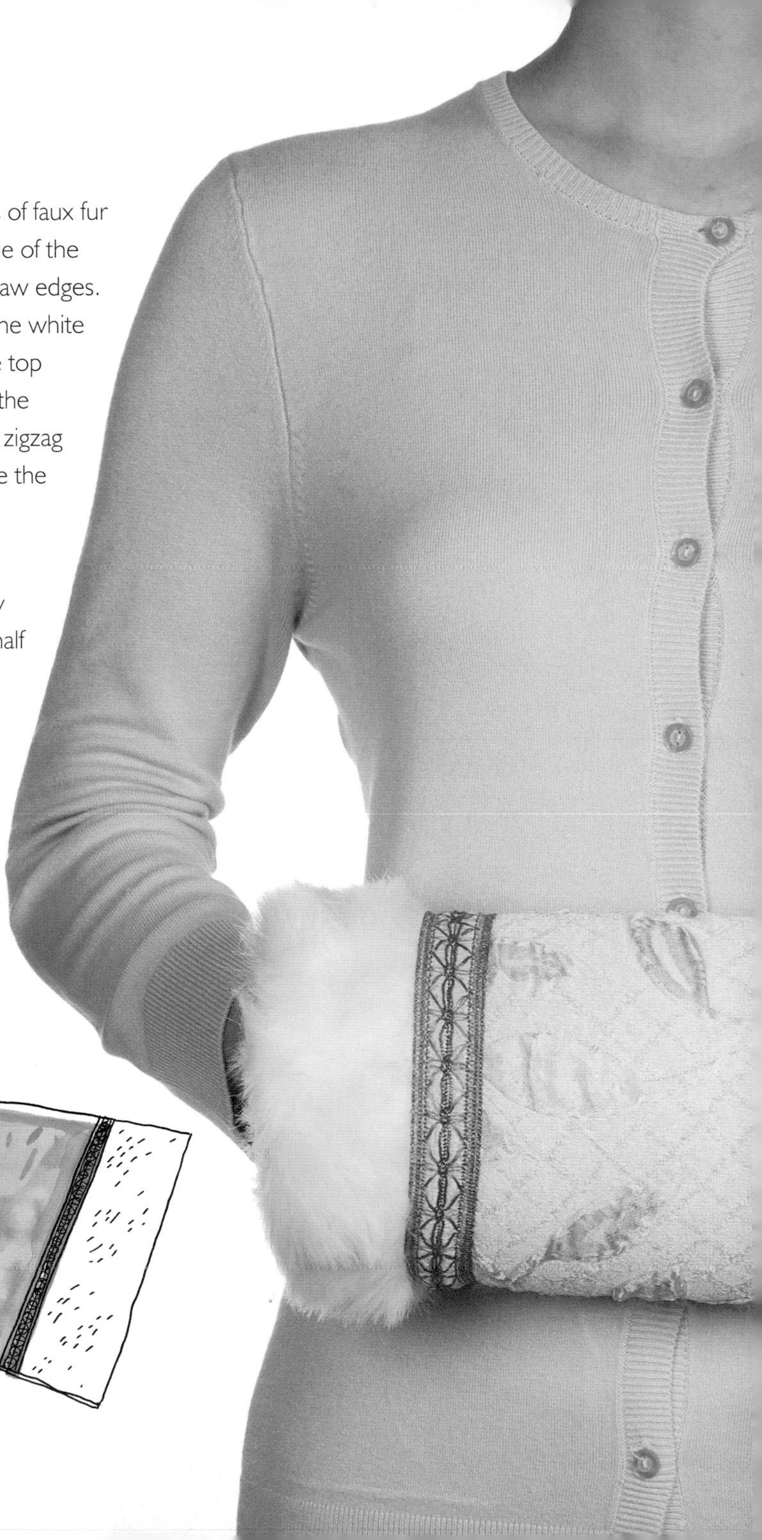

3 Pin the piece of faux fur cut for the back to the pieced top with right sides together. Sew around three edges, leaving one of the short ends open. Note: Faux fur tends to stretch as you sew. You may need to trim any excess from the seam allowance.

4 Clip the corners (page 19), and turn the piece right side out. Use a knitting needle or a chopstick to push the corners out. If you notice that any fur is caught in the seams after turning, use a needle to pull it out and fluff it up.

5 Insert the foam, fitting it into all the corners. Fold the open edges in and pin. Then hand-stitch the seam closed.

6 Roll the piece into a tube end to end. Use the embroidery floss to stitch the ends together. Take long stitches, which are better for holding the bulk, and pull them tight. If needed use a needle to pull the fur free from the stitching and to fluff it up.

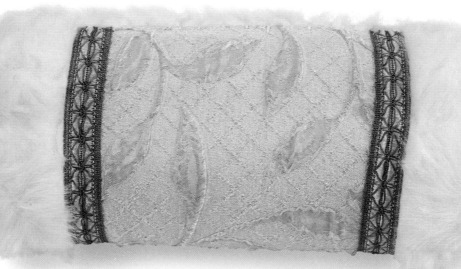

cuddle drops

$\mathcal{M}$ade using invitingly soft fleece and super sweet, candy-colored, recycled fabrics, these plush pillows are cuddle ready. Perhaps their contentedly closed lids will inspire you to indulge in a little snooze.

DESIGNER

ELLEN WRIGHT-SHAW

WHAT YOU NEED

Basic Pillows Tool Kit (page 11)

⅓ yard (30.2 cm) of fleece fabric for the drop

Scrap of recycled vintage/retro fabric for the face

Scrap of black felt

Thread to match

1 decorative button

Polyester fiberfill

SEAM ALLOWANCE

¼ inch (6 mm) unless otherwise noted

FINISHED SIZE

8 x 12 inches (20.3 x 30.5 cm)

WHAT YOU DO

1 Copy or trace the templates on page 113 and cut them out. Cut two drops from the fleece. Cut one face from the recycled vintage/retro fabric. Cut two eyelids from the scrap of black felt.

2 Place the face right side up on one of the fleece drops, centering it on the lower part of the drop (figure 1). Using plenty of pins to keep the shape from shifting when you stitch, pin inside the shape as well as around the edges.

figure 1

3 For a wide, bold line of stitching, set your machine for a wide, short zigzag. Sew around the edge of the circle. Then set your machine for straight stitching. Stitch two lines around the circle, outlining the zigzag stitch. Stitch one line on the outside of the zigzag, stitching over the points, then stitch another inside the zigzag. Set your iron to medium and press around the stitching.

4 Pin the eyelids to the face, and then edgestitch them around all edges. At the right eyelid, sew three straight lines coming diagonally off the side of the lid (figure 2). Drop your feed dogs to free-motion embroider a small circle at the end of each line. Position the button at the upper left of the other eyelid and sew.

figure 2

5 Pin the two pieces of fleece right sides together and sew. Leave a 3-inch (7.6 cm) opening at the bottom of the drop for turning. Overcast the seam using a zigzag stitch.

6 Turn right sides out and stuff with the fiberfill. Stuff until firm, adding small handfuls at a time and shaping as you go. Hand-stitch the opening closed.

FOLLOW THAT THREAD

Wondering where to find great old fabrics? Search your own closets and cupboards first. Look for pillowcases, bedspreads, table cloths, and clothing. To extend your quest, visit local resale shops, yard sales, and flea markets.

soft spheres

DESIGNER
VALERIE SHRADER

*L*ooking for that just-so Japanese zakka decorative accent?
Look no further than these elegant fabric balls.
Sew them up in multiples using Asian-inspired prints,
then display as a chic tablescape.

WHAT YOU NEED

Basic Pillows Tool Kit (page 11)

Fabric scraps

Thread to match

Polyester fiberfill

SEAM ALLOWANCE

¼ inch (6 mm) unless otherwise noted

FINISHED SIZE

3 x 3 inches (7.6 x 7.6 cm)
4 x 4 inches (10.2 x 10.2 cm)

WHAT YOU DO

1 Using the template on page 126, cut out six pieces, mixing the fabrics as desired.

2 Think of assembling your sphere from two pairs of three pieces each. To begin, stitch one edge of two pieces together, right sides facing. Fold the seam allowance back when you add the third piece, so you can see where the angles of the pieces align.

3 Make a second pair of three pieces as you did in step 2. Stitch each pair together, right sides facing, leaving an opening to stuff, and turn.

4 Stuff as desired. Use the slipstitch (page 25) to close the opening.

SUPERSIZE IT

You can enlarge or reduce the template as desired to change the size of the spheres.

pillowbox hideaway

$\mathcal{S}$nap open the top of this understated pillow box, and you'll discover a tiny hidden compartment inside. We think it's just the right size for late-night munchies or the remote.

WHAT YOU NEED

Basic Pillows Tool Kit (page 11)

16 x 22-inch (40.6 x 55.9 cm) piece of 2-inch (5.1 cm) foam

22¾ x 48-inch (55.9 x 121.9 cm) piece of quilt batting

¾ yard (68.6 cm) of microfiber

10 x 20-inch (25.4 x 50.8 cm) piece of upholstery batting

10 x 10-inch (25.4 x 25.4 cm) piece of buckram

½ yard (45.7 cm) of a silk print

¼ yard (22.8 cm) of a silk dupioni in a solid color

Craft paper

Spray adhesive

Paper-backed iron-on adhesive

Thread to match

Invisible thread

4 size 10 sew-on snaps

3-inch (7.6 cm) frog closure

SEAM ALLOWANCE

½ inch (1.3 cm) unless otherwise noted

FINISHED SIZE

10 x 10 inches (25.4 x 25.4 cm)

What You Cut

Foam
- *1 piece, 10 x 10 inches (25.4 x 25.4 cm) for the cube bottom*
- *2 pieces, each 6 x 10 inches (15.2 x 25.4 cm) for the sides*
- *2 pieces, each 6 x 6 inches (15.2 x 15.2 cm) for the sides*

Quilt Batting
- *2 pieces, each 11 x 48 inches (27.9 x 121.9 cm)*

Microfiber
- *3 squares, each 11 x 11 inches (27.9 x 27.9 cm) for the lid and cube bottom*
- *4 pieces, 11 x 11½ inches (27.9 x 29.2 cm) for the sides of the cube*

DESIGNER

JOAN K. MORRIS

WHAT YOU DO

1   Cut the foam, or have it cut for you at the place of purchase. Cut the fabric as described in the box, left. Copy and enlarge the two circle templates on page 128.

2   Build the foam box following figure 1. Use the 10-inch (25.4 cm) square for the bottom. Place the two 6 x 10-inch (15.2 x 25.4 cm) pieces opposite the 10-inch (25.4 cm) sides. Place the 6-inch (15.2 cm) squares between them. Following the manufacturer's instructions, use the spray adhesive to hold the pieces together.

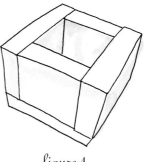

figure 1

3 Lay one piece of quilt batting on your work surface and center the foam box on it. Wrap the batting up two sides of the box and then to the inside. Pin in place. Center the box on the other piece of quilt batting and repeat. Tuck the corners under to miter and baste (figure 2).

figure 2

4 Center the buckram on the length of upholstery batting. Wrap the batting around the buckram and hand-baste the ends together. Set aside.

5 On the paper side of the iron-on adhesive use the circle pattern to trace five each of the 7-inch (17.8 cm) and 4½-inch (11.4 cm) circles. Cut the piece of adhesive to separate the larger circles from the smaller ones.

6 Lay the piece of adhesive with the 7-inch (17.8 cm) circles on the *wrong* side of the silk dupioni, and the piece with the 4½-inch (11.4 cm) circles on the *wrong* side of silk print. Follow the manufacturer's instructions to fuse the fabrics. Cut all the circles out.

7 Center one of the 7-inch (17.8 cm) circles on one of the lid pieces, right sides up. Remove the paper backing and adhere. Then center one of the 4½-inch (11.4 cm) circles on the larger circle, remove the paper backing, and adhere.

8 On each of the four side pieces, position a 7-inch circle (17.8 cm) 1 inch (2.5 cm) up from the 11-inch (27.9 cm) bottom edge, and centering it between the sides. Remove the paper backing and fuse. Center one of the smaller circles on each of the larger circles and fuse.

9 Make a bobbin of the matching thread, but thread the top of your sewing machine with invisible thread. Set your zigzag stitch for a medium width and short length. Zigzag around the raw edges of *all* circles.

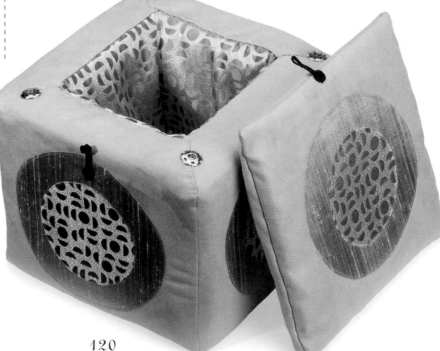

10 Pin the two lid pieces right sides together. Stitch around three sides. Clip the corners and turn right side out. Make sure to push out the corners. Slide the batting-covered buckram inside, fold in the seam allowances on the open side and hand-stitch closed.

11 Make the inside box lining for the cube. Cut five 7-inch (17.8 cm) squares from the remaining silk print. Pin them with right sides together to make a cross, then stitch (figure 3). Pin the sides with right sides together. Sew up from the central square, leaving ½ inch (1.3 cm) unsewn at the top of each seam. Press the seams and turn right side out.

12 Make the outside cover for the box. As you did for the lining, pin, then sew a cross with the 11-inch (27.9 cm) square cut for the bottom as the center piece. Sew up the sides, leaving 3 inches (7.6 cm) unsewn at the top of each seam. Clip the corners, press the seams, and turn. Slide the foam box form inside.

13 Slip the lining in the box. Pin the unsewn ½-inch (1.3 cm) seam allowances around the top edges of the foam. Fold in the top corners of the covering to miter and pin (figure 4). Fold the top edges of the covering under and pin to the lining fabric. Hand-stitch all in place.

figure 4

14 Sew the large snaps to the corners of the lid and box. Pin the frog in position to the front of the cube and lid and hand-stitch in place.

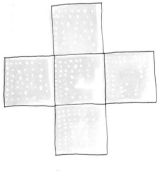

figure 3

CUT IT OUT

If you want to cut the foam yourself, use an electric knife and your job will be done in no time. Just make sure to keep your precious pinkies well out of range of the rapidly moving blade.

templates

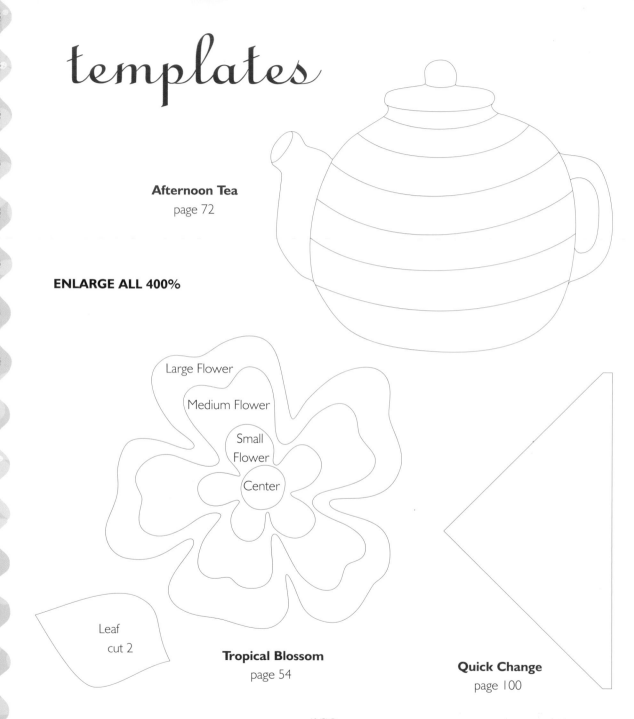

Afternoon Tea
page 72

ENLARGE ALL 400%

Large Flower

Medium Flower

Small Flower

Center

Leaf
cut 2

Tropical Blossom
page 54

Quick Change
page 100

Two-Tone Truffles
page 66

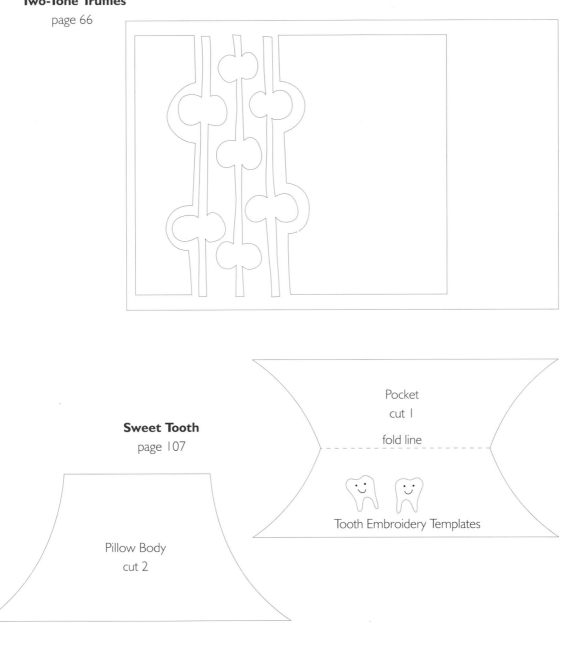

Sweet Tooth
page 107

Pocket
cut 1

fold line

Tooth Embroidery Templates

Pillow Body
cut 2

ENLARGE ALL 400%

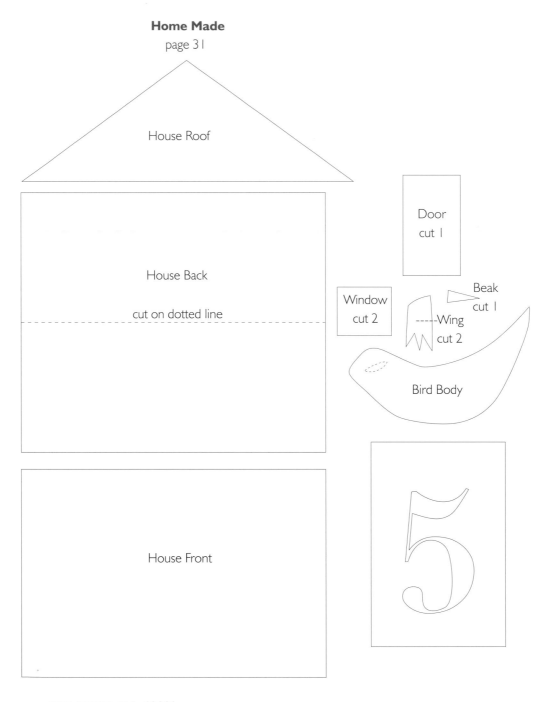

Home Made

page 31

House Roof

House Back

cut on dotted line

House Front

Door
cut 1

Window
cut 2

Beak
cut 1

Wing
cut 2

Bird Body

5

ENLARGE ALL 400%

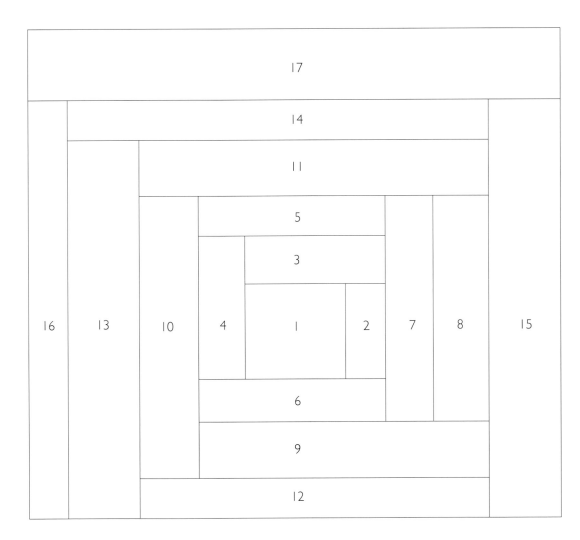

ENLARGE 300%

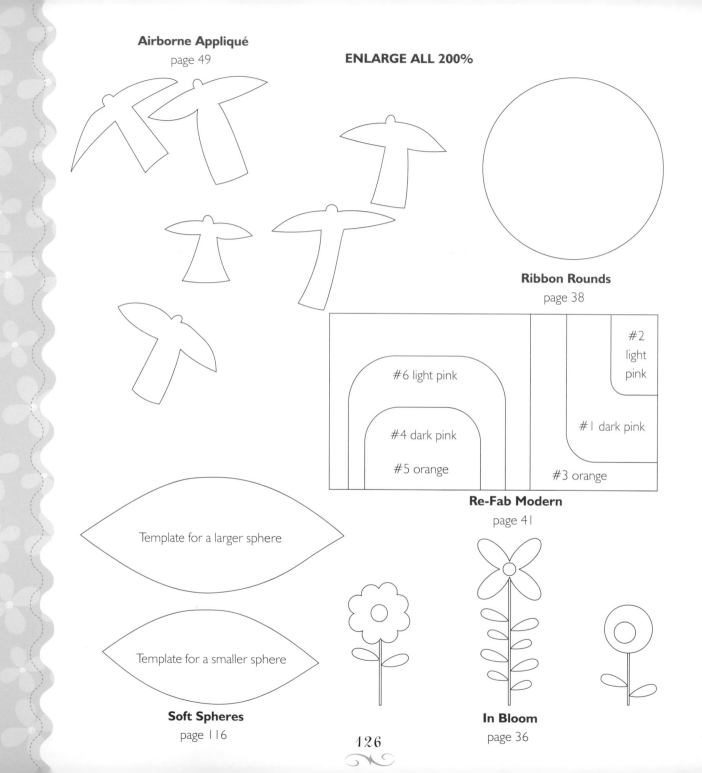

Airborne Appliqué
page 49

ENLARGE ALL 200%

Ribbon Rounds
page 38

#6 light pink

#4 dark pink

#5 orange

#2 light pink

#1 dark pink

#3 orange

Re-Fab Modern
page 41

Template for a larger sphere

Template for a smaller sphere

Soft Spheres
page 116

In Bloom
page 36

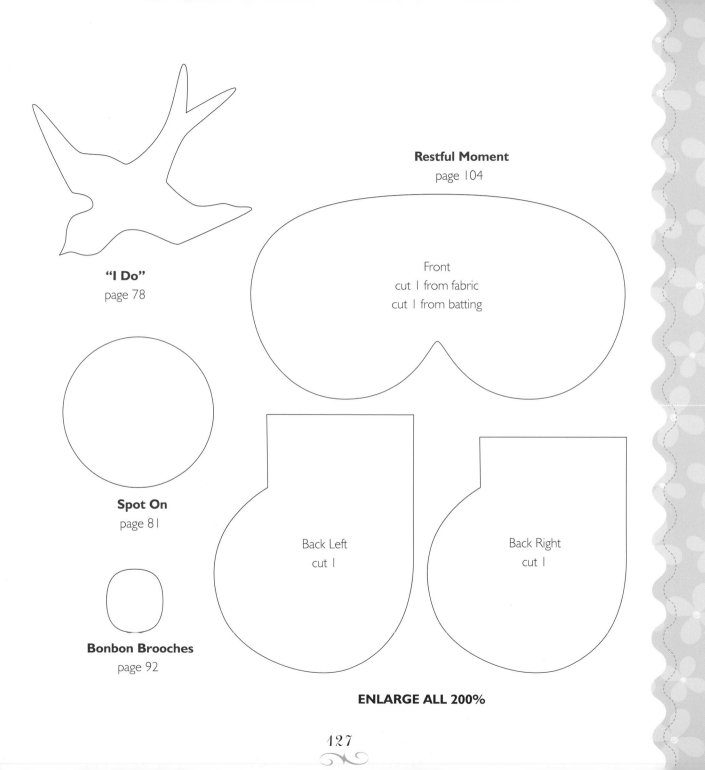

"I Do"
page 78

Spot On
page 81

Bonbon Brooches
page 92

Restful Moment
page 104

Front
cut 1 from fabric
cut 1 from batting

Back Left
cut 1

Back Right
cut 1

ENLARGE ALL 200%

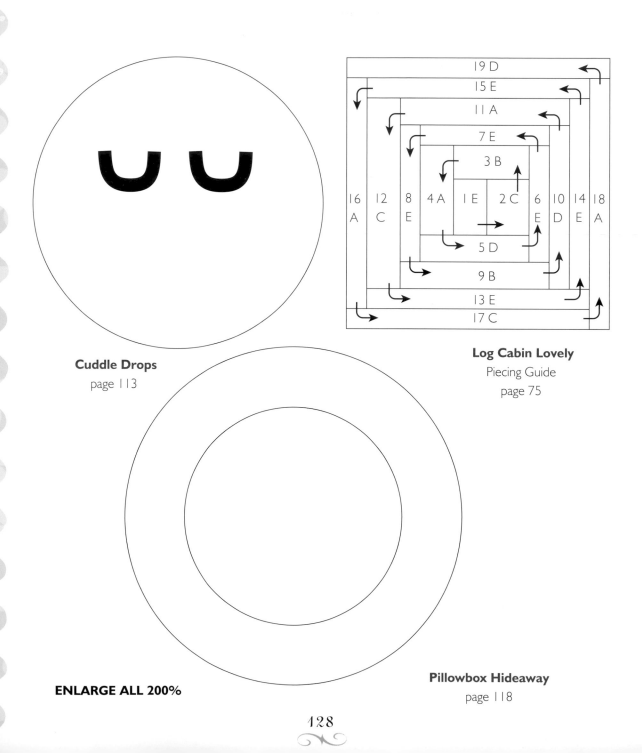

Cuddle Drops
page 113

Log Cabin Lovely
Piecing Guide
page 75

				19 D					
				15 E					
				11 A					
				7 E					
				3 B					
16 A	12 C	8 E	4 A	1 E	2 C	6 E	10 D	14 E	18 A
				5 D					
				9 B					
				13 E					
				17 C					

ENLARGE ALL 200%

Pillowbox Hideaway
page 118

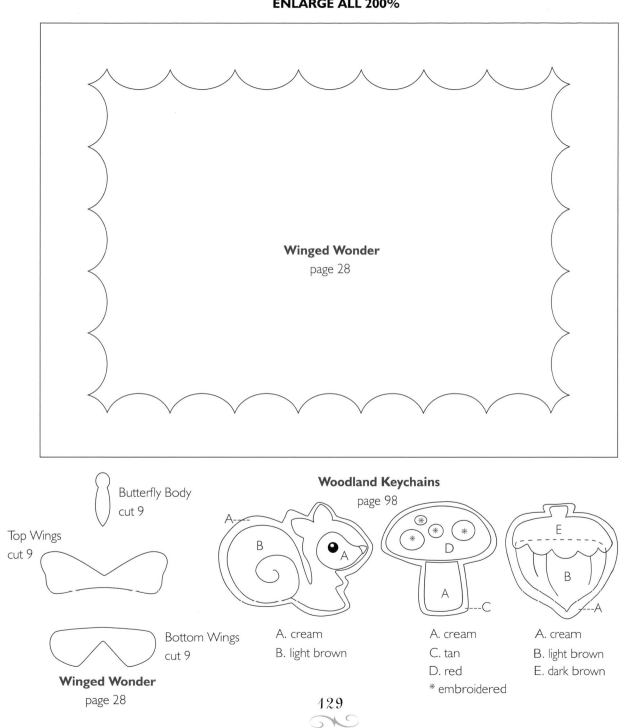

Winged Wonder
page 28

Butterfly Body
cut 9

Top Wings
cut 9

Bottom Wings
cut 9

Winged Wonder
page 28

Woodland Keychains
page 98

A----

B

A

A. cream
B. light brown

*
* *

D

A

----C

A. cream
C. tan
D. red
* embroidered

E

B

----A

A. cream
B. light brown
E. dark brown

about the designers

AMANDA CARESTIO is an editorial assistant with Lark Books by day and serial crafter all other times. She keeps herself busy with various stitching projects, stained glass, and costume-oriented pursuits, although she's constantly tempted to try new things. See more of her stitched creations in *Pretty Little Mini Quilts* (2010) and online at www.digsandbean. blogspot.com.

JENNIFER COOKE is a graphic and textile designer. Her company, Raeburn Ink, is an ongoing exploration of pattern and color in the form of printed clothing, accessories and home products. Her work has been featured in *Lucky*, *Time Out New York*, *Nylon*, and *New York* magazines, and she has designed exclusive products for Urban Outfitters and Patagonia. More information on her work can be seen on her website, www.raeburnink.com.

MALKA DUBRAWSKY is known for her hand-dyed and pattern fabric work and has recently turned her attention to crafting quilts, pillows, and other sundries for sale via her online store, www.stitchindye.etsy.com. She is the author of *Color Your Cloth* (2009). Her work has been featured in several publications including *Quilting Arts* magazine and *Quilts, Baby!* (2009).

YVONNE EIJKENDUIJN was born and raised in The Netherlands but traveled the world and now lives in Belgium. Yvonne is a homemaker, photographer, and shopkeeper. She writes about her home and lifestyle at www.yvestown.com.

CASSI GRIFFIN specializes in unique designs inspired by nature and vintage children's books. Her designs can be found in numerous craft books, including *Pretty Little Pincushions* (2007), *Pretty Little Purses & Pouches* (2008), and *Craft Challenge: Dozens of Ways to Repurpose a Pillowcase* (2009). She chronicles her adventures at www.belladia.typepad.com.

AMANDA HANLEY is a graphic designer working in Boston, Massachusetts. Her work has been sold in small boutiques and online venues. Along with sewing, she is an experienced crafter, artist, and mid-century collector. Visit her design and craft blog at www.redjetwhistle.blogspot.com.

ELIZABETH HARTMAN is a self-taught sewer, pattern designer, and crafting enthusiast. She has been developing sewing patterns for quilts, bags, and household items. She lives outside Portland, Oregon. Visit her blog and Etsy site at www.ohfransson.com and www.ohfransson.etsy.com.

NATHALIE MORNU works as an editor at Lark Books. She's the author of *Quilt It with Wool* (2009), *A Is for Apron* (2008), and *Cutting-Edge Decoupage* (2007). Her next book is *Leather Jewelry* (2010).

JOAN K. MORRIS' artistic endeavors have led her down many successful creative paths, including costume design for motion pictures and ceramics. Joan has contributed projects to numerous Lark books including *Pretty Little Pincushions* (2007), *Pretty Little Potholders* (2008), *Button! Button!* (2008), and many more.

TIFFANY ANN NELSON is a first-generation, self-taught quilter. Her passion for beautiful fabrics fuels her desire to open up a fabric store where she can encourage others to create. She calls Atlanta, Georgia, home. You can visit her online shop at www.warmnfuzzies.etsy.com.

KAREN PHILLIPS is an art teacher with a dual passion: photography and sewing. She knew she wanted to be an artist from the age of five and was greatly influenced by both of her grandmothers, who were artists and quilters. Her business, Shutterstitch (Shutter for photography and stitch for sewing), can be found online at www.shutterstitch.com.

AIMEE RAY has been making things from paper, fabric, and clay for as long as she can remember. She is the author of Doodle Stitching (2007) and Doodle Stitching: The Motif Collection (2010). She has contributed to many other Lark titles. You can see more of her work at www.dreamfollow.com.

LEESA RITTELMANN is an art historian who lives and teaches in upstate New York. She has been designing and sewing for more than ten years. Inspired by a variety of modern and contemporary artists and artisans, her designs are still cranked out on her grandmother's machine. For examples and inquiries visit www.flickr.com/photos/square1studio.

VALERIE SHRADER is an editor at Lark Books and has written and edited many books related to sewing and needlework. She knits every now and then, and hopes that art quilts will be her next creative exploration.

RUTH SINGER is a British textile designer-maker who creates bespoke and limited-edition textiles and accessories using organic and vintage fabrics. She is a skilled textile historian and uses traditional hand-sewing techniques to create unusual textures and sculptural effects. She is the author of Sew It Up (2008). You can find out more on her website www.ruthsinger.com.

CATHERINE THURSBY embraces a variety of forms of creative expression, including painting, jewelry making, sewing, and sculpture. She has fulfilled a lifelong dream by opening her very own shop, Red Shoes, in her hometown of Ann Arbor, Michigan. Visit her shop at www.redshoeshomegoods.com and read more about her life at www.redshoesllc.typepad.com.

Born in Finland, KAJSA WIKMAN is very fortunate to be able to work full-time and whole-heartedly as a crafter. Her company, Syko Design, has come to represent playful art textiles characterized by her childlike drawn doodles translated into fabric and thread. Her work can also be found in Quilts, Baby! (2009). Find out more at www.syko.fi.

ELLEN WRIGHT-SHAW has had a passion for color and design as long as she can remember. She is greatly inspired by vintage fabrics, graffiti, Japanese culture, and children's drawings. Find out more at www.melon1.etsy.com.

acknowledgments

It took many people to make this book look as good as it does. Thanks, first of all, to the talented designers who contributed their imaginative and beautiful projects to this book. A big round of applause for sharing your brilliant talents and inspiring us all!

Thanks also to Lark Books' dedicated editorial team: Nicole McConville and Beth Sweet. Megan Kirby's art direction provided a beautiful setting for the book's words and images, and Jeff Hamilton's art production made it all come true.

A final thanks to those who helped make the book as lovely as it could be: Susan McBride for her sweet illustrations, Orrin Lundgren for his masterful patterns and templates, and Steve Mann and Stewart O'Shields for their skilled photography. Finally, thanks to our outstanding cover designer Celia Naranjo, and talented models Meagan Shirlen and Shelly Schmidt.

index

It's all on www.larkbooks.com

Can't find the materials you need to create a project? Search our database for craft suppliers & sources for hard-to-find materials.

Got an idea for a book? Read our book proposal guidelines and contact us.

Want to show off your work? Browse current calls for entries.

Want to know what new and exciting books we're working on? Sign up for our free e-newsletter.

Feeling crafty? Find free, downloadable project directions on the site.

Interested in learning more about the authors, designers & editors who create Lark books?